# Mama's Putting You Up on Game

## GRACE CHANG PIGGUE

ISBN 979-8-88616-694-1 (paperback)
ISBN 979-8-88616-695-8 (digital)

Christian Faith Publishing
832 Park Avenue
Meadville, PA 16335
www.christianfaithpublishing.com

Printed in the United States of America

A memoir for my beloved daughters

# INTRODUCTION

My dearest Aubrey and Ava,

I am writing this because one day, you will experience many emotions and feelings, and I want you to remember to embrace it, enjoy it, and learn from it. I want you to embrace it even in the hard, painstaking times because that is when you learn and grow the most. So look on the bright side, for the harder and more painful the situation, the more you grow and learn. It's like a muscle—for it to grow, it must tear and endure pain; yet in the end, it has more capacity and strength.

Initially, I wanted to put y'all "on game" because I wanted to try to protect you and make sure you experience love in the most beautiful way. But that is impossible because only Jesus can do that and God's plan is the best plan and His timing is utmost impeccable. All I want to do is share some things with you so that when you go through it and should you ever feel alone, you'd know Mama went through it too. Truth be told, we all do at least once, and I want to also help you embrace those moments and give you validation. Everyone feels differently about these moments, even for similar experiences; still, that doesn't mean that one's feelings are right or another's are not. Rather, it shows how we deal with these experiences and what we get out of them can also be very different.

Lastly, I do not know where life will take us, and I cannot guarantee I will always be there physically or be ready emotionally to hear you go through these things or whatever it may be. I hope we would always be transparent and feel safe and secure, knowing that we will always be there no matter what we are going through. Still, things happen, and only God knows what is best.

Through fasting and spending time with God, I know He has truly given me a vision—for me to show you what I felt and experienced, what kept me going, and what voice inside me led to where I am today. So I hope we are always honest with one another and truly listen to each other. You guys also have each other, but you are very different and will have very different emotions and react differently, and it may be hard to relate to one another.

I know the foundation of Christ is in you. Yet there will be distractions and obstacles. One can only control oneself and one's reactions. I pray I can help guide you in becoming confident in yourself and learning to be true to yourself and put God first above all so that, in turn, it will help you make a choice you know in your heart was true to you. Although many say, "listen to your heart," I've learned that you need to be able to differentiate what to listen to—whether your ever-changing emotions, meaningless societal ideals, or the never-changing and everlasting Holy Spirit in you.

# PART 1

# Mama's Humble Beginnings

Where should I start? I do not want to bore you with my humble beginnings; still, I feel like that is at the core of who I am today. It is why I am who I am. My childhood was so different from yours, and it is important I share it with you. As you know, Mommy was born in Toronto, Canada, but Halmoni (my mom and your grandmother) and Halbi (my dad and your grandfather) finally decided to leave and migrate to Montreal, Atlanta, and finally to sunny SoCal. We left behind Halbi's family in Toronto (Halmoni's family lived in South Korea, and Halmoni left there to Canada and met Halbi) with that move. It was a move that no one understood, not even our families, but Halmoni made up her mind, and loyal Halbi followed. I later learned it was a calling from God. Halmoni's pure faith in Him inspired the seemingly irrational decision to leave a pretty settled life and a huge loving family. With Halbi and believing in the calling, she left with a 5-year-old and a six-month-old to settle in Los Angeles, making random stops on the way.

I barely have any memories from Montreal and Atlanta. However, the few I remember are not very good ones. For example, I remember not enjoying preschool or daycare and being anxious as a young child because I did not like it there. For some reason, I remember vomiting but again not sure if it was at school or home and what triggered it. I remember having to be forced to learn and speak French, and maybe that was too difficult. I am not sure exactly

1

what made me feel these ill feelings, but I know I was not comfortable. Therefore, it ached my heart when I had to leave you guys at preschool all day. I know you both had a challenging time, especially for you Aubrey because you were forced to nap because you had to be there longer hours. I even hated seeing other kids being there all day away from their parents.

As a society in the United States of America, we have become numb to the idea of taking kids away from their parents so young. A parent should not have to return to work after six weeks and be separated from their children so early. And we wonder why kids have anxiety, separation issues, and emotional distress. If only we unfold the layers, then we would see what is at the core. I believe it is important for kids to go to school and learn to become independent. Still, it is disheartening to see kids reaching out to their parents when they are dropped off at daycare because parents have to go back to work. Those first couple of months to years are so vital and should be spent with your baby. It may also decrease postpartum depression and other mental states for both the parent and child. I do not have any research data behind these hypotheses, but I am sure there are some out there. I once read this meme that said, "They want working moms to work like they do not have kids, yet mother like they are not working." And this is so true. We are constantly battling *guilty-mom syndrome*, what I have begun calling it where we are trying to be both and yet feeling we are not *enough* at both simultaneously.

We need to support super parents trying their best to be great at working and being parents. Or provide support when making a choice to halt one to fulfill another. I understand it was not my reality or the reality of most parents, but if it did change, it could be impactful for the future of how our children are raised and, in turn, change our societal norms and expectations for the better. Lucky for you girls and me, I was very lucky to have Halmoni, who watched both of you until I thought you were ready to slowly attend preschool.

Sorry, I got sidetracked. But prepare yourself because I will do a lot of that throughout; beware. Still, I will always come back to where I left off.

Let's start from the City of Angels which, honestly, in hindsight, makes so much more sense as I feel like it truly is a city of angels. Los Angeles was great, at least my memories of it. We lived in Koreatown, where I made my best friends and played Chinese jump rope or *gong gie* (five pieces of circular objects we would throw and catch in a specific sequence) during recess and lunch. All was well in Koreatown, and it was here that I had some awesome experiences like having my first crushes and going to Washington, DC. Oh, I remember feeling emotions for boys. Yup, innocent feelings like blushing when we speak or playing truth or dare while low-key, hoping it would be something with him, totally innocent. A particular recollection I have from our entire amazing and educational visit to Philly or Washington, DC, was when our class was walking on the streets, and Levi's (my first real crush in Koreatown) best friend at the time tried to purposely block him from walking next to me. Although his friend was talking to me, I remember thinking how odd it was for him to block Levi from standing near us. Unfortunately, I do not remember anything else such as historic sights like seeing the Liberty Bell but such a minute insignificant incident. I have no idea why, but it shows that emotions and what the experience made me feel last more than actual visual memory for me. I mean, if I saw pictures, I can probably relive some of the moments, but this one moment stood out without even a picture to look back on. Who was Levi anyway? Levi was my first crush in fifth grade. I remember feeling a little flattered and yet a little confused that his friend even did that in the first place. Probably nothing serious, just all fun and games, but again a weird memory because it was a feeling I would never forget.

I remember when holding hands was a huge move because it rarely happened. When it did, it was for a few seconds because you couldn't hold hands for long because your hands would get sweaty. And since you do not want him to know you have sweaty hands, you'd take a break (wipe the sweat off) and reach for his hand again when you're ready. I don't even think we ever even kissed. It was so pure and innocent. It was "love" to me at age eleven. I remember buying Levi a yoyo for Christmas, I think (yup, yoyos were definitely a thing), and excited to give it to him because it was our first gift exchange. I also remember liking the funny guy and the mysterious guy but, again, all just feelings of an emotional preteen. By the way, I will touch upon these boys later.

At the time, I did not realize this, but my first crushes as a preteen were all Korean guys, including Korean pop groups such as H.O.T. and g.o.d. There was also a singer called Seven, a rapper named G-Dragon, and the singer who sang really a high pitch, yet looked so masculine—oh and, of course, Korean actors from beautifully written and produced dramas. My all-time favorite has to be *Autumn in My Heart*. Literally, I stayed up all night to watch all the episodes via VHS (you will never know what that is). Anyways, it was in 2000, and it was the first romance drama that not only melted my heart because of the handsome actors but moved my heart. It signified and portrayed what I believed was *true love* at that time in my life.

It may seem a little weird that I mention that my first crushes were Korean, but I realize race/ethnicity was and is kind of a big deal. Korean stuff is super cool now; everyone loves Korean BBQ, K-pop, Korean skincare, Korean dramas, etc. But back then, it wasn't. I mean, it was who I was, where I grew up, and what I stood for, which was totally normal because it was the same for most of my friends and the people living in Koreatown. But it was definitely not put out there like a fad and not even close to where it is now. There was no prejudice or racism—not that I noticed—because most of my peers at my school were either Korean or Hispanic, and we were all cool with it. We would bring stinky Korean banchan for lunch, and occasionally, we would eat the free meals at the cafeteria—meals such as calzones and pizza. Did you know that back in the day, we actually looked forward to some of the school lunches? I know, so weird. I remember the lunch tickets and how you could not forget them if you wanted to get lunch. I look back and think, wow, I felt like I belonged, and for good reasons. We all had similar backgrounds, Korean, probably mostly first generations, and hardworking parents. I cannot say middle-class family looking back now, even though at the time, I did not feel like we were struggling. However, we were not middle-class and were definitely getting by with the grace of God.

Halmoni and Halbi left Canada, our home, to start from scratch. They were not professionals like doctors or lawyers, so they literally "started from the bottom, and now we are here" (sorry, you know I love Drake, who is also from Toronto, and had to stick that in there). I want to emphasize this because although I knew we were not well-off, at that age, it was not a big deal. It was what it was. We lived in a one-bedroom, one-bath apartment that I remember as clear as day. We lived down the street from our elementary school, and since Halmoni did not drive, we walked everywhere. Luckily, everything was so close, including our church, which was important because church was the foundation. It felt like our whole life revolved around it. For one, we relocated to Los Angeles for this particular church, and since we left our entire family and the church we attended was a small church, it soon became a part of my family. We also had these cool white trucks that sold everything from candy and chips to bananas and vegetables. Most of my peers either had similar backgrounds or a little better or maybe worse; I never really noticed. Life was pretty cool. I bring up race, socioeconomic status, and financial situations early because I now look back and see that they were pretty significant determinants of how it molded me into who I am.

## First glimpse of racism

My first experience of racism was as a child. Before that day, I had not noticed White folks because there weren't many in my area. Before this incident, I felt no difference when it came to various ethnicities. We are all humans...and as our church would say... "we are all sinners, and God sees us all the same." I believed it. I believed we, humans, were all created equal and only God can judge us. But, man, was I wrong. I remember this old Caucasian man. He looked like he needed to shave or just had that scruffy look. If I remember correctly, he did not look mean or anything in particular. We were walking home—my little sister, my mom, her friend, and her daughter, who was also my friend, and me—with the women chatting behind us and laughing out loud. I mean, they were just being middle-aged women, probably talking about normal daily stuff and happy they could confide in one another and enjoy what we now call mom life. We were just being kids walking in front of them and playing when I heard a man's voice yell something along the lines of "Shut up! And go back to your country!" I do not remember my age exactly, but I was old enough to feel this emotion inside me. I got bloodshot red in the face and embarrassed for my mom and the lady. Yet my petite mom, your Halmoni, did not skip a beat and turned right in his direction and yelled back, "You go back to your country, you son of a ——!" I literally went from embarrassed to so proud of my mom for not only standing up for herself but for all of us. I was also surprised by how much history she knew about this country because we all know Christopher Columbus wasn't the first man to set foot on this land. This is a whole other story.

Anyways, that was one of my favorite memories of Halmoni. I am not condoning yelling and cussing out people who are being ignorant or mean. However, it made me look at Halmoni a little differently. Before that day, Halmoni, to me, was another stay-at-home mom who depended on her husband to make money. Her job was to take care of the kids and make sure food was ready. I loved Halmoni, but I did not really like the idea of dependency. I thought that if something happened to him or worse, if he wanted to stop working and stop taking on this huge responsibility, what would happen to us? But after that day, I realized my mom was smart and must have had other reasons to have been in that situation. It is not that it is bad to depend on a man, but I discreetly envied those who did not depend on nobody/man. Although my dad, Halbi, was an epitome of a good man—a man of God, hardworking, loyal, and an ideal father—I did not like the idea of dependency. I think it is because I learned early on that God is the only one whom you depend on 24/7. Everyone else always falls short. However, I should not have completely disregarded people and, in turn, hardened my heart.

Halmoni and Halbi were not perfect, still not perfect. I remember hearing arguments between my parents. I do not remember exactly what the arguments were about, probably the typical arguments many married couples have—money and infidelity. Who knows? But I would pretend to be asleep, and I would hear their words. And I remember crying secretively, making sure your Emo (your aunt) did not wake up as she slept next to me. Yet I would cry myself to sleep. I would sometimes pray and talk to God. First, I would be angry like, "Oh my goodness, why did they even get married or have kids." I even vividly remember hearing them say one time that they will stay together until the kids are grown and then part ways as if this was now a business deal. I felt like a burden; I would sometimes go to sleep and tell God, "If I do not wake up, I will not be mad but happy because I am in heaven with you—the one who always loves and never sees us as a burden." I was embedded with the beautiful thought of heaven, of how there is no pain, no shame, no more suffering. I love looking back now because I know at that time I physically did not have anyone, but spiritually, I knew God was with me. I spoke to Him directly. He saw my tears when I hid it from the world. He saw my hurt when I tried to bury it deep down. Honestly, I look back, and I envy my child's faith. I need to be like that more than ever. I need to just talk to Him straight. I need to surrender and raise my hands and tell Him, "Jesus, take the wheel," like Carrie Underwood. Halmoni and Halbi did do one thing right, and that was drilling the importance of having Jesus.

You see, being raised at the church has its pros and cons. One of the pros is I knew I always had God to talk to. Jesus was the only "man" I could 100 percent depend on. I knew He was the only one that would not disappoint or fail. I also knew heaven is home, and this place called Earth is not permanent, so to me, death was beautiful because it meant no more pain or suffering. I did not fear death. I recall actually saying to Him that once I closed my eyes to sleep that I would be completely at peace if I woke up to be in heaven. I know it sounds a bit like I had some mental health issues and probably needed and still need therapy and counseling. I do not think it is healthy for a young child to be thinking about death. Trust me I know heaven is the only place where there will be no more suffering, but I thank God every day that he took those thoughts I had and made them disappear by morning. I thank God that somehow, those were just thoughts and never an action. I do pray and hope that you will never feel some of the feelings I felt, but we are all human and will all face challenges and trials. I just pray that you will turn for help. I was very young, and mental health was not a hot topic, especially not for children. I am glad the times we live in now are more accepting and more prepared to help young children in these areas. However, in the end, I know the only reason I was able to overcome those thoughts was because of God. It did not happen overnight as it is a process, and it will continue to come up throughout this memoir and my life.

Another thought I grew to have was making a list of everything I would never do if I ever had kids. I know it sounds so dramatic and a little crazy for an elementary-school-aged child to create a list of all the things I would never do when raising my own child. I wish I saved the list because I am sure it would have given me a clearer glimpse of how I was feeling and good insight, but it was thrown away a long time ago. It could have also helped me be a better parent as I reflect upon what I was feeling and going through. I remember writing things like "never fighting with your husband even if you think they are asleep because guess what, they know what is going on, and they are probably listening." I also remember writing something about "not sharing how much money you do not have with your child. Let your child be a child and a little carefree and not have to worry about the bigger issues, at least not yet." I know it sounds so depressing, but as I reflect, I want you to know I am glad I never made you guys feel that way; at least, I hope you didn't. I want you girls to know you are lucky because that feeling is typical for many children. For instance, I remember spending the night at an *unni's* house and hearing her parents fight. I mean, they fought on a whole other level. I felt bad, yet my *unni*, someone I looked up to like a sister, was so strong. After that, my outlook changed a little. I knew I was not the only one, and that there are far worse situations. I am not saying these incidents are okay, but we are all human, and unfortunately, many people have disagreements, and children can get exposed to the good and bad of them. I also want you to know that I am not mad at Halmoni or Halbi but so grateful for these experiences because they made me who I am today, a woman who puts God above all, who only trusts in Him and who will always turn to Him first.

## Halmoni and Halbi

Over the years (I am fast-forwarding only this part), as Halmoni and Halbi were active members of the church, God truly worked through their marriage. As time passed, they fought less, and now, I know they no longer fight, and they have love for one another. I think I knew because of their love language, which is acts of service. When Halbi was in the hospital and had open-heart surgery, we were all very stressed and overwhelmed. Still, I tried to hold it together, especially since you, Aubrey, were only three months old. It was a challenging time; I was in grad school, just had a baby, and my father almost died. Your dad was amazing, but again as you know, I do bottle up my emotions pretty well and sometimes release them in a very peculiar way like running or working out. Anyway, as a family, we learned a lot about our family dynamics, and most of all, our faith was tested. In the end, our faith won; thank God. However, this was also the first time I witnessed the love between Halmoni and Halbi, and it somewhat brought healing into my heart, knowing that all those years of struggle were worth it because I knew they had true unconditional love. It is hard to explain, but when for most of your life you think your parents are not *in love* and are bound because of their kids and marriage under God, you start to think it is nothing more than an obligation. I am not blaming anyone or the situations, but this probably brought a little trauma, and it may have affected the way I saw *love*. Yet nothing is permanent; everything changes, except God. So to see that although it may have started with love and became troubling in the middle, ending again in love was beautiful. God is love.

## Back to K-town

Another vivid memory I have in Koreatown was when I was in grade school and had cut-and-paste activities but no glue. I am not sure if it was a financial thing, or we just did not have it. Either way, I remember using white rice (yup, go figure). Halbi brought a fresh bowl of rice and showed me that getting a little bit of sticky white rice and squishing it in between my index finger and thumb made a tacky glue-like substance that we smeared on the paper. It totally works! I was a little embarrassed at the time, but now I love sharing this with some of the parents I work with because it shows how resourceful a parent can be for their child's success.

The last memory is the hardest one and one that still brings tears to my eyes. I remember I would get money as gifts from other adults, and I would save it. I do not know what I would save it for, but every time it became a large sum, I would always end up giving it to Halmoni and Halbi. It began with them asking to borrow it from me but me, always knowing exactly how much they would have in their bank accounts, I would gladly give it to them without any question to pay rent or whatever we needed. As long as I remember, I knew exactly how much they had, when Halbi got paid, and when bills went out. There was no room for anything in between. I am not sure exactly when I started to know how much they always had, but it may be because they were always talking about it. I was partly being nosy and also trying to help.

Hindsight, it was probably best not to know because it was just another stressor that I had no real control over. You mature real quick when you start hearing how much rent is, how much groceries are, and figuring out what is left. The only thing I made sure I never did was put more burdens on them by asking for things. No one believes me, but we never had a Christmas tree growing up. My first tree was also your first Christmas tree. First, we were always at church for Christmas. Second, we never had those gifts under the tree like how it is normalized. I am not telling you this to feel sorry for your Emo or me; I am telling you so you are forever grateful for being able to experience those early childhood joys. Joy is a choice, and like peace, it can only be provided by Jesus. I am forever thankful we chose joy and did not have any ill memories. I pray you are always grateful because we sure were. I was never sad about it, at least not to my knowledge, because it was not normal to have all that in the first place. I never watched commercials saying, "Oh, I want that," and I never asked for those things because I never wanted your grandparents to feel guilty that they were not able to purchase those items for me. They were doing the best they could with what they had, and I was grateful. These are the very memories that keep me humble when watching you guys open your wrapped presents from your family, especially from your grandparents, every Christmas. We spent ours celebrating the birth of our Savior, Jesus Christ, and I am very grateful for that because Jesus gave us salvation and because of Him, we have no sin and able to go to heaven. You are fortunate to have the best of both worlds, and I pray it continues.

## The move

I had a great deal of love and connection to Koreatown and to the community. I loved being able to walk to Koreatown Plaza and meet with my best friends and buy Sanrio pencils and some small clear stickers that look like what we may now call emojis. I remember buying stationery to write letters, going to the music store, and listening to all the songs via headphones before being 100 percent sure I wanted to purchase the CD, a compact disc. There was no YouTube, Pandora, Spotify, or device that played all your favorite music in one sitting. You had to buy the entire compact disc (CD) of the artist you wanted. I remember going to the ice cream spot in the food court and walking over to my friends' houses and meeting halfway because we all lived so close and walking alone without a phone was not putting yourself in danger. I remember the hot Cheetos from the ice cream truck that sold it with melted cheese, and so a fork was necessary. I remember meeting up with some of the boys and going to the café and ordering *bapbingsoo* or going to my friend's house to play Chinese jump rope. I remember going to Samantha's house and using her computer to log into AIM (AOL instant messenger) because she had a computer. Those huge computers were our first big thing before cell phones, texting and DMing but are now obsolete. Funny to think now, but you couldn't use them while using the phone at the same time. Boy, times have changed.

Everything was great until I found out the news—the worst feeling ever. We were moving from Koreatown to a random city I had never heard of. When I was told we were moving, I was devastated, distraught, confused, to say the least. I felt it happened so fast. The decision and the actual move flew. Only about forty minutes away, still I was in a totally different world. I went from fitting and belonging to being the only Asian female in my entire elementary school. I was not taking count, but it sure felt like it. Anyhoo, on my first day, I remember Mr. Gee sitting me right next to the only other Asian person I can remember. Great, so the only two Asian kids were sitting right next to each other; what a coincidence. He was nice; I was just not in the best mood for a long time because I hated that I moved.

Real quick, even after we moved, Halbi and Halmoni felt bad because I just got into a renowned, gifted class, and you had to get tested to get in. So for about five months, we commuted. I would wake up bright and early, and Halbi would drop me off early, which was perfect because I had other extracurricular clubs such as guitar lessons that were provided by the class before school started. Then after school, I was part of all the fun clubs, like Shakespeare. After all that, I would walk home with Samantha. Samantha's mom, who was a nurse, would make us delicious Korean food to eat, and we would be off to do homework or play outside or just talk until my dad came to pick me at around 6:00 p.m. or 7:00 p.m. Yup, that was what it was for about five months. I am forever grateful to Samantha and her family because they allowed me to be in their home during that time. They fed me and took me as part of the family even though they had a lot going on. Samantha's dad was a pastor, and she had a younger brother, so it was a busy household, even without me. Yet they knew the great opportunity to be in this class and wanted me to take part in it even if it meant some sacrifices on their part. I will always appreciate their kindness and love.

It was a lot for everyone, especially for Halbi. I hated seeing him fall asleep on the wheel. I would literally sit in the back and give him the hardest shoulder and back massages, and yet he would still end up falling asleep. I knew he had a long day, and I was making it longer, but I could not give it up. I loved going to school there—I got a part in the play, had a crush who supposedly liked me back, and was starting to get the hang of learning eighth-grade English and Math. I am not exactly sure what level the teacher taught, but it sure was not fifth-grade level. He was going through MLA format and everything. I knew it was good for me, my future, and my parents' future. However, it was not worth seeing my dad tired and almost getting into car accidents every other night. So I gave it up. I was devastated. I cried and cried. And even though I had friends call me every day to fill me in like I never left, it was already different. I did still get to stay in contact with my crush, Levi, and of course, when I would come to visit my best friends, I would try to somehow see if he would be around and innocently meeting up at the mall or the Koreatown Plaza. It was nothing crazy. Halbi and Halmoni knew, I think. Surprisingly, they were always very understanding. I think at that age, you literally just wanted to be in one another's space aside from class and feel a little independent and grown up.

Eventually, I moved into my school of residence where my little sister, Emo, was already attending kindergarten. I came in the middle of fifth grade, which sucked since everyone was pretty much set—they had who they hung out with, who they liked, who they did not like, etc. I went to school trying not to get too emotionally attached. My heart was truly still in K-town, and any chance I got, I was out there. Here meant nothing to me, and I did not want it to. I will be honest; I probably did not give off the best vibes or attitude because it was hard to mask my disappointment. Yet I tried to suck it up and take it one day at a time. I quickly learned the Asian-girl stereotype—smart, nerdy, goody-two-shoes, etc. I mean, in my other class, getting the correct answer was hard, so it was looked upon as a positive. Not like a "brown noser," a term I learned at this school from the students. Oh, how I hated this school, but I slowly tried to not get all the correct answers as I learned quickly that being the best scholar was not cool. I also quickly realized that I just left a highly gifted class to a regular fifth-grade class, so I needed to just chill. I did not need to prove anything to anyone. I already knew I was at grade level or above; not to sound snobbish, but we were doing algebraic equations and reading and comprehending Shakespeare at my previous school. Obviously, most of my classmates knew that I was probably a high achiever and made fun of me for it. I do not think they meant to hurt me, but I was different from most of the peers, and it was easy to call it out. It was what it was.

Also, I had culture shock as I went from being in a fifth-grade class where even the notion of liking a boy was worth giggling and gossiping about to a place where boys and girls made out with their tongues—yes, open mouth—in the yard during recess. I know, gross. *Where in the world did they even learn to do that?* I would literally think to myself. I could not even imagine kissing a boy, better yet, with an open mouth and exchanging saliva. Double gross, but kids were doing it, and it intimidated me. It intimidated me because I did not want to get there and hoped that I would never have to. Yes, I definitely was in a doozie.

For a long time, I felt out of place, resenting my parents for the move. I wish I kept my journal from when I was going through all this to prove how strongly I felt. But all I have are memories of what I felt, some of which I tried very hard to erase. I loved our church and the community, but I honestly did not understand why it relocated to a city with literally no Korean people. I did not understand how the church would actually make an impact or how our pastor and his wife were dealing with decreased attendance, new community, and more. I just did not understand and was very unhappy. Looking back, I sound very selfish. Everything was about me and how I felt. I did not even take a second to think about how it may have affected others or even think about how it may have been God's will for the church, which included me. I know it sounds like nothing, but that move was a huge deal for me. I would cry and vent to my best friends in Koreatown and would visit as much as I could. However, I remember feeling so terrible that at night. I would literally talk to God and say, "If I do not wake up, I will totally be happy because I will be in heaven with you." Sound familiar? Yup, the move was that devastating. The change, the new environment, and not having anyone to really talk to about it in person was a lot. You see, I had friends, but I did not have an older sibling or an older cousin to confide in. Maybe that was on purpose, but I do recall wanting someone to talk to. You see, all of our cousins were either in Korea or Canada, and I did not have an older sibling, so I had to figure it out on my own with Jesus by my side. It probably did not occur to Halmoni or Halbi or anyone else what that big move did to me or what it can do to a kid. I mean, a kid cannot possibly feel lonely, hurt, or just have mixed emotions just from change. But it does, and I am sure it takes a toll on kids every day. Just this reflection hurts me because I know children are forced to adapt and be okay with change.

With students, or just people in general, consistency is key, and so attempting to grasp how traumatizing change can be for a child makes me cringe.

Once you become an adult, you forget these feelings, these moments you had as a kid, and sometimes disregard a child's feelings. I am totally guilty. I see you and your sister sometimes crying, and I am angry because you look like you are just crying for no reason. I do not take the time to ask why, and when I do, I do not think the answer is valid. Sometimes I get angrier and try to teach you to brush it off and be more assertive, but was that the right thing to do? I do not know; I am no expert at parenting. All I know is sometimes I feel bad; I feel bad for making you stop crying and for not validating your feelings, whether it is something silly like wanting the purple cup and not the pink cup or genuinely feeling bad for hitting your sister.

Either way, I blame myself, and I am sorry. I think I was programmed early that tears meant weakness, and feeling sad is pitiful; you cannot possibly just have a bad day and cry it out. Being sensitive was not a characteristic you wanted. So I swallowed a lot of my tears or quietly cried myself to sleep, hoping God would hear my tears once again... Sound familiar?. I would literally have the worst thoughts like, why was I born, why was I placed in this situation, and I questioned God a lot. At night, on my bad days, I cried out to Him, asking, "Why am I here and for what?" Imagine such deep and yet crushing thoughts, and I wasn't even a teenager yet. I did not like many parts of my life because we had other issues like financial and residency matters, and the move just amplified it. I know soul-crushing thoughts that I would never ever want you to think or say. I am very grateful that those thoughts were just thoughts, and I never acted on them. I am lucky I had my faith in Jesus and prayer, and as I went further, I found peace and understood that His plans are truly greater than mine. "And we know that in all things God works for the good of those who love him, who have been called according to his purpose" (Romans 8:28) is one of my favorite verses.

Through the faith Halmoni and Halbi showed in Christ, I learned to trust Him and love Him unconditionally. If He makes sure the birds and animals are fed and have a place to sleep, He surely will do more for His beloved children. I believed it. Jesus made miracles happen, and I believed it. If He can do those miracles, surely, He had to have a plan for me. However, if you or anyone you know is thinking horrible thoughts, or worse, wants to act on those thoughts, you need to reach out for help. There are many resources now, and mental health is real. I wish I had other venues and outlets to ask for help, but thank God the foundation Halmoni and Halbi placed in my heart kept me anchored. I pray you girls never get there, but I am sharing this because it happened to me, and I know it is happening now to many young kids. You think what is happening to you is the worst thing ever; you think only you are going through it, but this is never true. I am not saying what one may be going through is not as bad as the next or that there are far worse things than your situation. All I am saying is feel what you feel, express it, talk to someone, and know God is always there. Do not try to escape from the feeling or ignore it. Yet know feelings and thoughts are not always the truth, nor stable, but the Word of God is the truth yesterday, today, tomorrow, and forevermore.

# PART 2

# The Transition

One of the most important things that was revealed was how obedient my parents were to the words of God when He said, "Pack your bags and move," and they did. He said, "Devote your time to the church," and they did without any bitterness. He said pay tithe, and even though they did not have much, they obediently gave His 10 percent back to Him along with offerings (Luke 16:10). From the outside looking in, it looked absurd. Why would people devote so much time, money, and effort to a *church*? Trust me, I did not get it. I was even embarrassed at times to tell people how many times a week my parents would be at service or doing something for the church. I should not have been, but I quickly noticed that it was not a typical thing. At times, I think I felt they put the *church* before the needs of their own kids. I did not understand. Yet as a parent now, I would not say it was the church, but it was Jesus they put first. I also realized that if my parents were involved and dedicated, it pulled me in too. Without knowing, I was helping—raking and sweeping leaves in my rollerblades along the driveway of our church and trying to stir up some worship when we did not have organized group leaders for our kids' ministry. Most times, I hated it and was ashamed. As I got older and realized socializing with peers is way cooler than helping clean the church, I got out of it immediately. However, looking back, I think hours of sweeping until I had blisters in between my fingers and "serving" in whatever way necessary was good for me. I learned that it is not what He can do for you but what you can do for Him, a lesson of service and serving others before you. It can be a cultural thing, but I think it's a Jesus thing.

Slowly but surely, I realized that what I thought was the worst thing to ever happen to me in my youth was probably the best thing that ever happened. It did not take long before I met some friends and moved on to middle school with them. I was still *nerdy*, but I definitely felt a little *cooler* and slowly feeling a little better about the situation and myself. I think being in that new environment sort of changed me. Not sure if it was the people, the environment, or if it was inside of me all along, but I started to become a little different from who I was in K-town. My friends in K-town also noticed, and I did too but did not take note of it as I thought it was just part of growing up. It was part of growing up, but it was more than that. Now remember those innocent crushes I had on those Korean guys? Well, it still stuck, and I felt there was unfinished business (I know, so weird). I told you I changed, right? I went from being super shy to initiating and calling these boys and trying to meet up and hang out, in a very innocent way, like at a boba spot to catch up. Remember Levi? Yea, I really wanted to catch up with him. One night while I was visiting Samantha, I called him on his house phone because no one had cell phones yet (I know, wild), and his mom answered, and I somehow ended up inside his house. His mom was super sweet and remembered me. But imagine how crazy I probably looked when his older sister and Levi walked in. Thankfully, his sister was nice, and luckily, I did not scare him off. I honestly remember feeling like, *Wow, maybe I am a little too aggressive. What the heck was I doing here? What if he does not even like me, and here I am, hanging out with his mom? What if he has a girlfriend?* Super awkward and embarrassing thoughts rushed in. He walked in and got super red in the face, but he was a good sport. He did not make me feel crazy, and we hung out, talking about sports cars, which we both were into at the time and, of course, our memories in fifth grade. I am not going to lie. It kind of felt surreal; just hanging out with a guy I liked in his room, like in the movies (not Korean dramas). It made me feel grown but also glad I made a move to call him. My aggressive and vulnerable move was worth it. I decided to walk back to my friend's house, but his mom made him walk with me. It was lovely; he was really sweet. If I remember correctly, that was also when my parents, your Halmoni and Halbi, met him. I was petrified but kind of excited because my parents had obviously never met a guy friend I had a crush on. There were mixed emotions but again a memory linked to what I never felt before and left lasting memories.

Afterward, at night, we talked on the phone, talking three-way or four-way with my best friends and maybe a guy friend of his. We went on a few dates, like going to the movies at the mall with our other friends. We were never just alone, but it was definitely a wonderful experience—that young, pure innocence, crushing on one another. Maybe we slipped in a kiss or two on the lips but definitely without any tongue. I hope you guys have fun and experience innocent dates and opportunities like this where you sit next to your crush at the movies and share popcorn and save those movie ticket stubs because he *bought* it for you. It was cute and sweet, and I am excited for you girls to also experience butterflies because it will be your first reciprocated "liking-ness." Liking-ness is probably not a real word, but what I mean is when two people like each other at the same time and place. Sadly, and honestly, I do not remember how, but it ended. Maybe he remembers, maybe not, but I know it was not a bad ending. No hurt feelings, no bad blood. And just like that, I moved on.

Forgive me if some of my timelines are off. I've realized how much I've forgotten about certain incidents in my life and how my mind really did a great job of trying to delete all the "bad" memories. I added this part because I found some memorabilia items I saved into a plastic container rather than a shoebox. Yup, it had items like old pictures from these places we went to take *glam* shots and my prom ticket. You are probably wondering, what are glam shots? It was a studio with backdrops, and you could choose one and go with whoever you wanted to take pictures, sort of like the family pictures we would go take, but these can be taken at random. Trust me, I have a few that my friends and I just matched and would go take pictures and then pass those pictures out to friends with cute messages on the back. It is pretty embarrassing to think about, but I loved that I kept them all, even the ones where I am just like, why? Anyway, it was like going down memory lane for real. I, unfortunately, tossed all the love letters, grams, and sweets notes when I got engaged to your dad and moved in with him, so these were the only few things I kept.

Well, in this box, I realized a few things. One, I was definitely 1,000 thousand percent an emotional preteen/teen. Two, I definitely forgot many details about my elementary/middle school life. For example, I liked a boy who lived across the street from my house. Well, apparently, I really liked him. I honestly do not remember details or any memory of us even hanging out, but I wrote like twenty *poems* about our little relationship—I could not believe my eyes. I used the word *love* way too many times, and he *hurt* me multiple times. I wanted to laugh at myself when I went back to read all of it. However, I did not because I could tell that my feelings were raw, and I genuinely liked this guy, and he must have really hurt my feelings. I remember my neighbor liking him first and how I felt wrong for liking him when I found out he liked me. I can see through that notebook how torn I was, but I went with my feelings. I wish I could say going with my *feeling* was a good decision, but it obviously ended in a disaster, and now reflecting, I wish I had really thought about my actions before acting upon my immature *feelings*. I sound so pessimistic, but here is what I gathered from the notebook:

1. My friend liked him first, and I should have stayed loyal even if he liked me and not her (chicks before dicks);
2. He had a history (not a positive one) that even at such a young age, it sounded like he has been a friend hopper (one who hops from one person to a friend of that previous person). That was definitely not a good look, so why did I assume he will change? Of course, I found out he did not;
3. Lastly, "the one" and *love* should not even be something I should be thinking about at that age.

I could not believe how invested I was in this boy at such a young age. Reading the notebook, I was so embarrassed that I wanted to burn it. However, I could not because those were some heavy emotions, and I needed to face them, hoping it would prepare me for what you guys may go through. With social media and everything being right at our fingertips, one can easily see just how big the world is, and I hope one advantage of that is that your maturity level will also have to fast-forward to keep up with the trends of the world; for example, dancing. When I was in elementary school, dancing did not look like dancing now, at least not for me. I did not have that good cable where I can watch women and girls dance on music videos and try to imitate them. Now, even at ages three and six, you guys watch YouTube and TikTok and learn new dances.

Also, I shared this story because I wanted to express that even though that "heartbreak" seemed devastating at the time, I have no recollection of any of the *good* or *bad* times I had with him. Although the notebook kept saying how "I'd cherish those memories," yet at thirty-three, I can honestly say I do not remember anything. I can barely remember what he looked like. So I want you to know, of course, I do not want you to experience any heartbreaks even at age ten; still, you will. But I want you to take it, embrace it, and then let it go. Trust me, girls, it ain't gon' be the last. All you can do is learn from it—take it for what it is worth and do better the next time. At ten, or however old I was, it seemed as though life would end but, girl, it didn't. The sun will come out the next day and that boy may have moved on and you may still be hurt, but I pray you do not keep any ill feelings but learn how important it is to truly understand your emotions and feelings. Now your brain has learned what emotions and feelings come out of a not-so-good circumstance, and hopefully, your brain has picked up on the warning signals, so next time, you will remember what the end-product was from that experience and will help you decipher your actions for future encounters. I think we ended up being friends later down the road. I mean, I do not remember holding grudges, and I saw my maturity and growth through that notebook, page by page. The beginning was just my emotions flying everywhere, but after the heartbreak and anger, I could see that I came to reality, and God must have transitioned my experience to a life lesson. I went from cussing to letting it go so that he can be happy, and ultimately, I could have peace. It also ended with chicks over dicks! I thought it was fitting because it started off as a bit of betrayal to my girlfriend, yet the outcome was boys come and go, but real friends stay for life. Just FYI, the friend and I never fought over him and never had any ill feelings toward one another and still keep in touch to this day.

## Wolves to buccaneers

I graduated from elementary school with one of the highest grades. I tried to hide it, but I was starting to own up to who I was, and doing well in school slowly became a part of me. I did have a few crushes in sixth grade and remember holding his hand at sixth-grade camp. Yup, we pack our bags and go into the mountains with no parents for a few days. I remember I practiced showering for only three minutes because I heard that was all the time you had. It was a bit romantic up there in the mountains with no parents. I mean, we had chaperones and slept in all-male or all-female separated rooms, but for many of us, it was our first time without our parents. Not me; I went across the country in fifth grade, but this was different as it was with a whole different group of people. I made memories and took lots of pictures. I am sure I still have them today.

Sadly, I do not remember much of it, but I know it all went well, and I remember who I liked at that time. Weird, right? I do not remember much in detail but holding his hand. This is how I know writing this is very important. I hope you share those moments with your sister or with me or just write them down. It may seem stupid at the time, but I am learning how the emotions of a preteen and teen are so intriguing and universal, and yet so different from one person to the next. Even if you were both there in the same room experiencing the same moment, it will all mean differently to each person. It's all perspective, and maybe one day, you will be able to share your perspective as I am now doing with you girls. Also, it is so weird that I do not remember what activities we did at camp or what we ate, but I remember holding hands with the guy I liked for brief moments when walking as a group through the woods. I believe it is because emotions leave lasting memories as I reiterated.

Like I said, I was kind of cool with where I was and the new friends I made. The transition to middle school was exciting because it was new people, new teachers, and a new environment. Also, our middle and high school were on the same campus; I know, right? I did not think that was odd until I became a parent with daughters. I probably would never put you guys in a school with this sort of arrangement, as you will find out later why. Anyhoo, I had a great time in middle school aside from what most kids went through, like puberty, awkwardness, and of course, "dating." I put it in parentheses because it was obviously not real dating once you are older and looking back. However, I do not ever want to discredit any feelings I might have felt or any experiences I endured. Middle school was great as I began to fully get to know myself—I learned to see what I liked and didn't like. I met some amazing teachers like Mr. L who literally branded me my nickname—Changster! I loved it and embraced it. He knew I was no gangster and had a head on my shoulders but also knew that this little Asian girl was no passive little girl. I felt like that nickname really started to grow on me like the rest of Bellflower. During this time, I began to "work." I put quotation marks in "work" because obviously, I was way too young to apply for a job and work somewhere. No, it was a cool after-school, during-the-summer type of gig.

Scarlett, one of my best friends at the time in Bellflower, had a dad that worked for a gym. It was a privately-owned gym, and so we started off as telemarketers and passing out flyers and calling people who wrote down their numbers for a raffle or who were once members and telling them about a new "promotion." Our job was to get them through the doors, and the rest of the actual staff would do their thing. You know those annoying papers you randomly find on the windshield of your car or door handle? Yeah, you probably would not because no one really advertises by paper anymore. Well, we placed those flyers on cars, and later, once we were older, we worked in childcare. I know it sounds crazy, but it was great for me because like I said, Halmoni and Halbi had enough on their plate, so I never wanted to bother them for anything I actually wanted; I was grateful that they provided what I needed. Mind you, Scarlett practically lived with me for some time and felt like a sister to me. Her dad was a person I looked to as a father figure also. He picked us up from school, took us to places like the mall or our friends' houses, and of course, got us our first job. It may not have seemed like a lot of money now, but we felt like we were balling back then. I got my first cell phone at the time and started to buy clothes that were cool and somewhat fashionable. Scarlett's dad helped out a lot, especially since Halmoni did not drive. He became my main source of transportation. I mean, I used to walk to school, but with Scarlett in the picture, we were picked up and dropped off. He was like a family member to me, except he knew when we would hang out with boys and who we were crushing at the moment.

One of the most important things that was ever said to me in middle school was by Scarlett's dad. I believe this was when we (Scarlett and all our girlfriend crew) became a bit boy crazy, meaning we were definitely *dating*, like going to the movies with guys we liked. He looked me in the eye via the rearview mirror and told me, "The greatest gift you can ever give your husband is your virginity." I know this may sound a bit random and old-school, but I was noticing people were moving in directions with boys that I was not ready for. He also knew how big my family and I were about Christ, so when he told me that, it stuck. It solidified the decision that I already made to God and myself. I was obviously not thinking about having sex at all. Still, it was good to get some assurance, outside my own folks, that what I believed and was taught was not *old-school* but actually *typical* ideals. I am not sure if I ever got to thank him sincerely for all he has done for my family and me, especially for those words, so "Thank you." Looking back, to me, it was the Holy Spirit speaking to me through him, just to bring me back centered at a time where I may have been drifting off.

Sorry I veered off again. Back to working and making money. Food was life. We ate what we wanted, bought what we wanted, and even bought the guys we liked things they liked. We enjoyed "taking care" of the boys we liked (yeah, that sounds so weird to say). I do not know when that started, but I think my love language started to come out.

We will talk about that later. Anyway, I remember we, my two best friends and I, would dress alike and match from head to toe. Yes, there was another best friend. We were like the Three Musketeers. We were always with one another. I honestly loved our time together. I mean, some of the things we did were a bit wild, but times were different, and I also knew God always had our backs. Unfortunately, I do not remember in detail anymore, but I do remember Limón Lays with Valentina sauce, bean and cheese burritos from the spot next to the liquor store, and boys. Oh yeah, I remember the boys. Sadly, I do not remember much of who my love interest was at the time or if I even had one, but I do remember theirs. Boy, it was great when it was great and the worst when it was bad. But again, we were in middle school, so honestly, what can you expect? No one knows what they want or do not want. I mean, we should not even have been thinking about long-term relationships, honestly. But I am grateful that through my friends' experience, I could feel what they felt and slowly began to see how a boy operates at that age.

Also, for the first time in my life, I experienced playing a sport. I loved sports and anything to do with physical competition, which I think I got from Halbi, who was a great soccer and baseball player. Just a little detour, but Halbi was actually so good that he was asked to represent a team to go and play in South Korea during his first year in college in Toronto. It sounded like a once-in-a-lifetime opportunity, and so he asked his professors and school, and they excused him. Well, he loved it and came back to school. The next year, he got chosen again, and this time, the school asked him to decide, and of course, being Halbi, he went to go play soccer. To my understanding, he never went back to school after that. I do not know the details, and I was a bit shocked to hear this story, but I knew he followed his dream, and for that, I admire him. I mean, if I could tell you his story of being raised in a third-world country to immigrating to Toronto, I know you would have tears in your eyes and look at your Halbi in a whole other way. Halbi had difficulty with English, but he was smart as a tack in math and even corrected his professors.

Because of his language barrier, getting a job was difficult, but he figured out ways, and once he was in the door, his work ethic shined through and kept him there and helped him excel.

Because of these stories and how hard Halbi worked, it built this drive and determination in me from day one. You see, because he was an athlete, Halbi would have loved to put me in sports, but he was always working and working late, and he never had the time or money.

## Money, money, money

Money... You girls are probably wondering, *Why were they always short on money?* Trust me, it was hard for me to swallow too, especially after moving to Bellflower. I was that one Asian girl, and I had to fit the stereotype—smart, nerdy, goody-two-shoes, and rich family. Except I was not the right fit. My close friends knew I was not rich and far from it, but they did not judge me because they came from similar backgrounds, with parents trying hard to provide. It was what it was. However, I always felt different from everyone else because of one specific thing. I think it separated me from many of my other peers, or at least we never spoke about it, so I am not sure who else was in a similar predicament. I want to let you know that we struggled because like I said, when we left Canada, it was not because we were getting relocated through Halbi's job or that Halmoni had a great career opportunity. Nope, I found out later it was a calling from God to Halmoni. Now at first, I did not believe it, but now I 100 percent do. We did not come with loads of cash when we came here like how some people envision Asian people do when they decide to migrate. They bring loads of cash and start a business or buy a home or both. Nope, we were like the other half and came just as is.

However, Halmoni and Halbi did the right thing and filed for our visas and green card, the correct legal way. I never understood why we would drive to downtown LA occasionally, pay for parking in a suspect parking lot, walk to a huge building, go through security, and meet with some man who was our lawyer. I remember waiting in a huge white room with lots of other people who were probably there for the same reason. It was a bit daunting. I mean, there were other kids there, but it was no place for a child. It was dull, boring, and anxiety driven because our parents were filled with anxiety, so naturally, we, the kids, did not feel comfortable. I will never forget the feeling I felt every time we would walk into that huge building. It sounds crazy, but it almost felt demeaning, like the US government was saying "your citizenship elsewhere is not good enough, and to be a US citizen, you must suffer and pay the price." From the first time I walked into that building until we finally got our green card, I felt that most *Americans* had this attitude where everything should be given to them as if they were privileged and entitled to get what they wanted because it is part of being an *American*. I viewed it as arrogance and hated it because I knew how hard many immigrants worked to get a working visa and/or a green card. Plus, everyone, whether you are from the United States of America or somewhere else in the world, should be treated the same because we are all human, and we should be treated the way we want to be treated. It is crazy because I have never actually told anyone how I ever felt about this. During that time, I was almost ashamed, ashamed that we were not *American citizens* and had to go through this grueling process. Yet because of this process, I have a stronger connection to immigrants and almost a disconnect with American citizens who feel because this land is *their* founding father's country, that certain things should be given to them automatically. Whereas others who may not look like them or sound like them or eat like them or act like them should be "taught, trained," and scrutinized and suffer a bit to see if they are worthy of being an *American citizen*. I know this sounds harsh, but I vividly remember that feeling, and again this is my perspective. I did not hate Americans; most of my friends were Americans, born in the United States of America. I just did not have the best feeling or memories regarding the immigration process and getting our green card. At first, I thought this was a normal process and that everyone could do it, but I soon found out why we were in debt and struggling. To go through that process, you need money and a lawyer, which means you also need more money and prayer because even if you played all the cards right, something could come up, and they can deny you. Well, let's just say it was a long process.

At some point, I wanted to shout to all my US citizen friends, saying, "Wow! You guys are lucky. You are just born here, and you do not have to go through this stupid process." I know immigration is a controversial topic, but to all the political people…us children did not choose to be an immigrant. Damn it! We did not choose to be born here or there. I know it's hard, but have some empathy, especially for the children. I understand that some people may feel threatened by immigrants or feel some type of way, but all I am saying is what would Jesus do? In hindsight, I now understand why God allowed me to experience this process.

Anyways, Halmoni and Halbi, my parents, continued doing it correctly. Even though not many people knew I was a Canadian citizen, I felt like an outcast, that and being the only Asian girl around. I am embarrassed to say, but I remember thinking, *Why am I ashamed of being from Canada? It is not like I am a fob* (fresh off the boat). However, as soon as those thoughts ran through my mind, I remember how terrible that sounded in my head. I was like, *Oh my goodness, it is working. I am turning on my own people and wanted to feel a little superior just because I speak English with no accent, and I am a Canadian citizen and not a citizen of South Korea.* I literally had to check myself. Is this what the immigration process, racism, being called Chinese, and having others make fun of my eyes all my childhood in *America* did to me? It made me feel ashamed of my roots and where I was from because that was not valued where I was; in turn, I internalized it, and I did not value myself.

## Understanding my identity

I do not recall ever feeling empowered because I was a Korean girl. It was not a topic in school, and it surely was not expressed in the media. I am embarrassed to say this, but I did not fully embrace my look until later in high school and almost in college. For most of high school and through middle school, I knew I was not considered "pretty." I did not have any of the characteristics of what defined beauty at that time. I think somewhere, somehow, *Asian persuasion* and this weird fetish of Asian women came about, which slowly made me feel like, wow, I may be considered "beautiful." Except it was more sexualized than what I wanted or expected, but again, as immigrants, we will take what we can get and don't make a fuss. Not going to lie; I was probably proud that finally, Asian women were now starting to get some limelight. Yet I definitely had to put my foot down like, "Nope, ain't no happy endings like that over here (I was not having sex or even getting close to that, and I let that be known)." I want to take a moment and inform you that I knew many young girls and boys that were having sex, obviously before marriage, and never did I judge them. I never looked at my peers and friends differently because of their decisions. However, all I wanted was the same. I did not want to be judged because I chose not to have sexual relations at this time. Yet even though many may have thought they were not, I felt judged and placed in a different category. I chose not to have sex for many reasons, but one of them was that I was not ready emotionally. I pray you never feel pressured or feel as outcasts because of any personal decisions, but I am sure it will happen because we are all human. I just pray in those moments you get your assurance from the Holy Spirit inside you. Holy Spirit will speak to you, but it is up to you if you will be obedient and choose to listen.

The beauty and pros of social media is that you girls get to experience and see that all that has changed and is progressing. Beauty is all colors, all ethnicities, all over the world. I love how it has diversified, and now everyone can feel accepted and beautiful. Beauty is not just on the outside but on the inside, and it is definitely not being judged by some biased old man somewhere. Overall, I think the media is slowly allowing people to see real beauty and expectations versus the facade.

I think I felt alone for many reasons and not seen. I did not have anyone to confide in and did not try; instead I bolted it in and continued to mask it. I did not know anyone in a similar situation as mine, and I was too scared and ashamed to share my story to see if anyone else understood. Now I believe that to want honesty and transparency, one has to be it first. Which is what I am trying to do with you girls. I hope you see my willingness and my vulnerability. Most importantly, I know God sees it.

Anyway, it just appeared that most kids I knew were more worried about the cute boy or the he-said/she-said drama, while I am contemplating my self-worth because I was not an *American citizen*, among other internal conflicts. I felt like none of my Bellflower friends could relate, and my Korean friends did know about my situation. It was like a weird yet touchy subject to me. I am not illegal, but I am not a citizen. I do not think kids my age would understand such uncertainty. Well, that uncertainty brought on unnecessary anxiety and shame. I should have brought it to God. No one should carry those burdens or any burden, especially not a kid.

However, because I felt like I was on that borderline (literally), I felt a deeper connection to immigrants in general. Technically, we are all immigrants; it's just some came a long time ago, some were forced here, and some are still dreaming of getting here. Yet now I realize the most important matter is...we are all here. It is beautiful to see and hear about movements like the Dreamers Act now that I am grown because it makes me feel like I was not alone. Still, no one talked about it, nor was it really looked upon as a positive.

I say this because I want you to be kind to all people—those who not only speak your language but different ones and especially those who speak with an accent. I literally hate when people would make fun of people with an accent. It hurt my heart, and yet I never stood up and said anything. I was again ashamed. Even something as simple as a friend calling the house (which you would never understand) and Halmoni answering bothered me because she would answer in Korean. The peer on the other line would then try to imitate it. I am not sure if it was to mock her or really trying to learn. Either way, I did not like it, and it brought an uneasy feeling in my stomach, a similar feeling I got when people would pull the sides of their eyes and make weird sounds as if they were speaking my language. Again, I remember the emotion I felt at each of these moments vividly. Even though the memories were not happy, nor exciting ones. I wish I could give perspective to everyone who ever made fun of a person who had/has an accent when speaking English, "Hey, at least they can speak two languages while you can barely speak one." I am not proud that I was so afraid, but I am here to show you to stand up for what you believe in even when it makes you uncomfortable. "If it does not make you uncomfortable, you are not doing it right," someone wise once said. That goes for most things in life. It makes me so proud when I see you girls trying to learn Korean words because I know for a while I was trying to hide that part of Grace, Korean Grace. I pray you girls will never have to experience feeling ashamed of who you are because God made you perfect. Jesus loves all people, and the one thing I know that this country needs to work on as a *Christian*-based country is one of the biggest things Jesus did and preached: love thy neighbor. Love everyone. No one can judge because we are all sinners, and no one is greater or superior to the other. I pray you never feel the feeling I once felt and that many people may have endured as immigrants but also know and understand what immigrants like your own Momma, Halmoni, and Halbi (your entire family) endured. I want you to be proud of your heritage and ethnicity and its roots, but also, I want you to embrace everyone. Whether they look like you or not, we are all God's children, "we all bleed the same" (by Mandisa), and once everyone understands that, I believe the world would spin a lot smoother.

I began to feel a little more at ease once I saw other Asians and other races from my middle and high school. Like I said, our middle and high school was one big campus, and it had all ethnicities. I mean, the majority was probably African American and Hispanics, but, man, we did have everything else in between, and I loved that. It was weird because although we were very diverse in race, everything was about our ethnicity. I do not think it was in a racist way, but I know I was known as the Asian girl for a very long time. I also remember it was a thing to know the race of the guy we liked or were dating. Race/ethnicity was something we were aware of, but not in a bad way. We knew we were different; we had different backgrounds, yet we all meshed beautifully. I think I loved that most about Bellflower. We also had this annual thing called International Day, where various clubs would showcase their different backgrounds, and I think that was when I started to fall in love with all the cultures except Korean. I know, that sounds weird, but there was probably a handful of us, and because we were so sparse, we sort of congregated with other groups.

Honestly, I was proudest to be Korean when I was in Koreatown with my Korean friends. It sounds bad, but no one I hung out with at school was Korean, so I could not indulge in our amazing culture or food with anyone. Instead, I hid it and pressed it down into my soul and would only let it out when I was in K-town. We would go to Jangtuh which, if I remember correctly, was like in August or September, and it was like those outdoor food marts that are now very popular, pre-COVID. I think it was like the first night markets I was ever introduced to. They had food, merchandise, entertainment, and more. I remember going and seeing all the Korean people, the Korean guys dressed in their Nike Cortez with spiky or slick back hair, baggy pants, huge white tee. I remember crushing on random Korean guys and thinking, *Wow, too bad ain't none of them in Bellflower.* I loved going to different cafés and *bapbingsoo* spots and trying different restaurants in and around K-town. I experienced my first concerts in K-town, seeing my celebrity crushes and howling their songs. I also remember walking the streets of K-town the year South Korea almost made it to the finals in the 2002 World Cup. It was a summer I will never forget. Everywhere you looked, there were Koreans dressed in Korean flags, yelling and smiling. Every lot, every plaza, they had huge projectors showing the games. Mind you, to watch these games live, you have to be up in the wee hours of the night because of the time difference. What a time to be alive! I honestly felt Korean Pride (KP). I began to have love and appreciation for South Korea, and although it took the men's soccer team to show up and put us on the map, it did way more than I ever imagined. I remember shortly after when non-Asian people would talk to me and find out I was Korean, they were in awe as though somehow, they thought I was related to the Korean men's soccer team, which made me feel accepted. Unfortunately, it was usually older people or people who watched soccer regularly and not from my high school. Most people in my high school did not follow the World Cup unless they played soccer. It did not matter because it lit a small fire that made me proud to be Korean. It also made me look at Korean guys again. Like, wow, they are actually *muh-she-suh*. It is a word I love in Korean because no word translates perfectly in English. It is a word that best describes when you are awed and impressed, like he just swept you off your feet but by his actions and not from mere lust and infatuation but mesmerized in an innocent and most doting way. Well, at least that is how I interpret the word. For a long time, I only described Korean guys with that word because I have only felt that way when seeing a Korean guy. I think I used that word a lot for Korean celebrities, especially in dramas, because many of their actions were just breathtaking. I mean that deep, unconditional, sacrificial love. It almost made you believe it can only happen in Korean dramas. I am sure I thought real-life Korean guys were like that too but probably from afar. Yup, I actually thought many of those Korean guys were attractive, but again I was only there for a night, and then back to Bellflower and to my reality.

I had some ideal views of Korean men; I mean, Halbi is an amazing man who has endured a lot and who I admire in many ways. I also had Samchoon (my uncle)—you may remember him, but unfortunately, he passed away on May 11, 2021. Samchoon was another Korean man that gave me a glimpse of what they are like. I think I may have viewed him a little different than most, but for some reason, I felt like I understood him, and my heart empathized with him. Like many Korean men, he had a lot of hardship growing up in South Korea when it was a poor country. Yet on top of that, he was born as Halmoni's half-brother. He had the same father as Halmoni but a different mom. Now it must have been truly hard living with your stepmother and half-sisters, probably not feeling welcomed and loved. He migrated to the United States before anyone else in our family and started making his life. He got married to a wonderful lady and had two kids. I am telling you his back story because I am almost certain it was hard, yet he never revealed that side to me. He never complained or seemed bitter. What he did instead was help us. I remember throughout my childhood that when Samchoon came to visit, it would be a great day. I knew it was going to be good because he always came smiling, and he either bought us something delicious to eat or always gifted us money, not like hundreds of dollars, but he would hand a twenty-dollar bill here and there. It sounds very simple, but having money as the main struggle made it feel like Christmas every time he came. Twenty dollars may not seem a lot, but back when I was young, I felt so blessed and lucky. You must understand the context. To a young girl who at times felt discouraged and bitter, he was a ray of sunshine. He was always laughing, and even though he may have had business issues or family problems, he never showed it to us. All he did was bring joy and a sense of hope, the hope that I too can succeed and will be able to pay back for all he had done for my family and me. He was the epitome of a *typical* Korean man. Halbi is too, but he is very different in a sense. I am not sure if it is because he never really displayed it or that his mindset is just a little different from most Korean men. Yet Samchoon, to me, portrayed it in every sense. For that, I am grateful because I think through him and Halbi, I respected Korean men so much more.

This part is just a special shoutout to my Samchoon. I wanted to speak at your memorial, but for some reason, something held me back. I also may have had tears flowing that would not let me finish my words, but I would have said something like this...

> Samchoon, I know we had a very special bond. You planted that seed very early in me. You would call me whenever you needed help regarding your business or just to say hi, and I was there without question. When you were going through your phase with difficult times, I hope I was enough. I hope you felt and knew for certain that I was in your corner when you felt no one else was. And I hope you never felt alone. I hope you felt loved even if no one was physically next to you. Thank you for calling me randomly to check on me and sitting down to have lunch with me. I knew your heart, and it was good. I know sometimes I may not have been the ideal person to talk to, but know that I felt every emotion and underlying feeling. I am so glad I got to know

you not only as my uncle but as a person. I am sorry that the last year of your life may have been the most difficult, and yet no one could really be present with you (because of COVID). I know it may have felt like you had a short time here on earth, but I know God took you early for a better reason. Yet I want you and everyone to know that you have impacted my life in only positive ways. I want to thank you. I want to show you that I will *choose* to be happy and believe even in the hardest of moments. I will remember my happy-go-lucky Samchoon as a tenacious, confident, and loving person. I could never repay you for all that you have done for my family and me. Still, I can live life remembering what it felt like whenever you came around and try to be that light and ray of sunshine to others, especially my family and friends. I am not sure how many knew your devotion and love for your family, but I did. I knew you loved being around family, just eating together and being in each other's space. I will also gather and spend time with our family as much as possible, even if that means I initiate every time—in your honor, as I know you would always bring our family together to eat and just be with one another. In the end, when I saw you in the hospital, I was so very proud of you. I was happy to see you vulnerable in front of God and to accept Him into your life again. It just solidified your faith, and it brought tears of happiness and a little sadness—happiness because I knew whenever He decided to take you, you will be right there in heaven; a little sad because I knew your time here on earth was limited, and there was absolutely nothing I could do to help. Your legacy will live on through your kids and others you have impacted. I will think of you and thank God for our time together. Until we meet again in heaven, Samchoon, feel free to show us signs from heaven as our angel, and you are welcome in my dreams. *Sa rang hae yo!*

## A melting pot of love

With time, I began to feel like I had a group I belonged to in Bellflower. I was valedictorian in eighth grade again, and this time, I thought I would be prouder than I was in sixth grade, but there was something that made me feel like I did not deserve it. Remember, I came from a *gifted* class? When I was in that class, I was not the smartest; I was probably average to low average in the class, depending on the subject. I remember struggling academically, yet luckily, my best friends were doing pretty well, so they helped me when I asked. So when I told them I was valedictorian, I distinctly recall one of them saying how even though I may be *valedictorian* at my school, it was not a great accomplishment simply because of who I was being compared to. I know my friend did not mean any harm, but that cut me and left a scar which, to this day, I battle with. I was hurt that she inadvertently put down the peers I went to school with and, on top of that, pretty much said if I was compared to "smarter, higher achievers," then I probably would not have been valedictorian. The main reason it stung was that I thought she was partly right. I knew that the peers at my school did not academically compare with the smart, ambitious, and rich kids at her private school. Yet I did not think her peers were better than mine, nor do I think she meant it that way. Like I said, she was my best friend, and what she said was out of love and her perspective. I respected my friend's point of view. Unfortunately, because she meant so much to me, and I valued her and her thoughts, I just began to think—and it planted another seed—*Maybe she is right*, I thought. I am not good enough elsewhere. Once, I met some of her peers and realized we were a part of two different worlds. She was right; I may not have excelled with such prestigious genes all around me. I questioned my own abilities.

I knew I was not intelligent or a genius, but I just tried really hard, especially with sports. I was not gifted with skills or talent, but I think God gave me heart and grit. I was always determined to do better. I brushed off what my friend said that day, but looking back, many of my own insecurities stemmed from there. Would I still be considered smart, driven, and college bound if I was at a different high school? Who knows? But I wouldn't change any of it because of the experience I received through my time at Bellflower. Bellflower taught me more than AP biology, and precalculus. It taught me the biology of my own body and what powers it holds. I learned that with the correct mentality of relations and functions, my body and mind can either come up with the wrong answer, or with God's help, it can be simplified to get the right response. I grew not only academically, but I matured emotionally. Bellflower taught me that being book smart is cool, but being street-smart and being aware was a necessity to survive in this world. I am also very glad that most of my peers were around the same socioeconomic status. We all came from humble backgrounds and knew we needed to work hard to make it. I believe that was one of the things that brought all of us together, in this melting pot. I am pretty sure it was right around this time I started to evolve. I think I slowly went from submissive and passive to more aggressive and confident. How I came to sports and my mentality on the court and field also shifted to being more positive, aggressive, and confident.

Sadly, my two best friends (the Three Musketeers) in Bellflower and I slowly drifted apart as well because we began to like different things. There were no hard feelings, but we just sort of dissipated into different groups. Scarlett played sports, so we were still hanging out a lot, but soon, she stopped sports and got into cheerleading. My other friend was not into sports but got into a different crowd. We would still have small talk here and there, but we were no longer attached to one another. We blossomed into our own selves, and we respected that about each other. No one can take away the memories or the bond we shared from elementary and middle school, but we also knew it was time to be our own person and let each other fly. I loved that.

We were mature enough to say "see you later" with no drama. Friends for a reason or a season like your grandma says. So I want to prepare you girls to also be okay with letting some friends go. It can be because of distance or just differences in interests. Still, at the end of the day, you have to respect one another and love one another, even if it means saying "see you later" and moving on from that friendship. You will have lots of opportunities to build friendships, trust me; I learned you can even make new and meaningful friends even at age thirty something. You do not have to hold onto that friend because you have known that person all your life. Some friends are meant for a lifetime, while others are not. God places people in and out of your life for a reason. Best believe that. However, it can be disheartening when you are young because you feel that friend should be your friend forever. Always be true to yourself and believe what the Holy Spirit is saying. Letting go is not a bad thing, especially when on good terms, and both parties understand. As I began to play multiple sports, I met new friends who also played sports, and they are my ROD/BFFs. Yup, those are your aunties. Aside from one, I met them all in middle school and have been BFFs ever since. ROD stands for Ride or Die, and yes, we took that title to heart. And the best part was I got to take all this right into high school.

# PART 3

# "The Game"

Let's get down to the nitty-gritty. You are probably wondering, *What "game" are you talking about, Mom?* Well, be patient. Without the back story, it will be difficult to digest.

High school was amazing—most of the time. I do not want to give you false hope because high school will be brutal; I mean, especially compared to elementary and middle school. I believe it is a pivotal point in your life. I now realize that high school years are the beginning stages to shape you to take on your early adult life. In hindsight, how I took on college, boys, and overall life obstacles after high school was a reflection of how I handled high school. It will make sense later, but I just want you to know I understand this time of your life is special and important as it will be a huge part of who you snowball into. No pressure. I just pray it will be just as fun as it is educational (academically, emotionally, and spiritually). High school is a big deal.

I told you our school went from middle to high school, all on one campus. I can remember clearly walking across the campus, ensuring I looked the best in hopes to possibly see my crush, some older, handsome young man. Of course, they would never notice a middle schooler like me because just as there were many gorgeous guys, there were just as many beautiful girls at my school. Still, it was always exhilarating to just stare in awe, and it never hurt to look and blush once you made eye contact and giggle with your girlfriends about it. I ain't gon' lie though; as I got older, the guys either decreased in charm and looks, or I realized they ain't much, which I pray you will quickly learn too, especially at this age. The looks are infatuating, but I am so glad I was not a head turner at a young age because I cannot imagine how easy it probably would have been to awe me with their *game*. So thank you, Jesus! But what I do worry about and partly why I am writing this book is because I know you girls will be head turners. You guys were already turning heads as babies, so I cannot even imagine. Everyone was so intrigued by your features and heritage. Your dad probably hit the gym harder than ever before, haha! I, in turn, prayed and wrote this for you guys.

## Here at last

Here, let me tell you about the one that put me on *game* or, in other words, allowed me to feel feelings I never knew existed which, in turn, helped me learn a lot about myself and how I portray relationships and *love*.

It's about my "first love." It's in quotes because it was love to me at age fourteen/fifteen years old, and I will call it that out of respect for my feelings when I was younger. Also, I referred to him as my first love for a while without revealing his name. I do not know why, but I did not like saying his name; maybe I was ashamed or afraid that too many people knew him. Whatever it was, I just referred to him as my first love for a long time. Anyhoo, I remember to this day the first time I noticed him. It is pretty hard to believe that it took until this day to notice him because I found out he was one of the star football players and fastest or one of the fastest (depending on who you spoke to) guys on campus. Oh, and I quickly learned a lot of girls had the hots for him. It was during sixth period, track practice, and I was stretching on the track and field as I was part of the track team my freshman year. The senior girls were the leaders and counting off our stretch, and I vividly remember one of the girls saying, "Okay, wait, hold on. I gotta see him."

I looked to see what she was talking about, and I literally thought to myself, *Oh, wow, you can do so much better. He ain't even all that. You are way too good and pretty for him.* I know, immediate judgment. Well, I knew the guy he was running next to as he was like an older brother to me, especially since my BFF, Scarlett, at the time was dating his younger brother. So that was how it began. I would hang out with them a lot and found out Titus was one of their best friends as he was always at their house. We did not hit it off immediately. I honestly don't even remember what it was that sparked it. I think he was a bit mysterious, and a part of me wanted to figure him out like a game and maybe I felt he was hurting inside or needed me. I know it's so weird that I felt this feeling. I am assuming it takes one who needs healing to know one, another reason why maybe *dating* at a young age is probably not always so healthy. Most grown people are trying to heal and make sense of trauma or whatever hurt they have felt. Yet young adults are also either still in the trauma or also trying to figure it out with less wisdom and guidance. Then you add on feelings and emotions, which sounds a bit dangerous.

Well, after a lot of hanging out, late-night talks, and wrestling, I grew to like him and truly cared about him. I felt like I got to know him like no one else did, no one else aside from his ex-girlfriend. At first, I am not going to lie; I was taken aback because they were each other's first, and I am sure they had history. Many girls, especially young ladies who are not sure of themselves and have insecurities, will always feel a little threatened by their mate's past. And it's totally normal; you have to understand that they definitely had some connection also. However, I do not think it is healthy to keep yourself hung up on that issue or compare oneself to their past because guess what; from the moment you start dating until you get married, the other person will always have a past and maybe some unwanted baggage that comes along with it, and so will you. So keep in mind... how much *baggage* do you want to have? It is your decision whether you will understand that their past is their past and ain't nothing you can do about it and just look to the future, or hold on to it and end up hurting yourself because you are worried about their past. It is a process, but so is everything else in life.

All I know is for me, I was never a jealous person from day one—a characteristic I have always had. I think it is my pride, and later added on was my confidence. I just was not about that feeling. Jealousy, to me, is a feeling you get because you are unsure of yourself. Like I knew what I brought to the table, and if homeboy was not about it and wanted someone else, I was like, "Please leave and be with her and be happy so I can be happy too." I can go into detail about that later. But all I know is one day, I was not worried about her or any other girl he had relations with. I grew less and less jealous as I grew more and more confident about myself. I also think as I got more mature, I realized I did not *need* him and would function perfectly, if not better (but trust this growth took a minute).

I felt we had a deep connection that no one else would feel or understand both emotionally and physically. We had late night/early morning conversations and meaningful understanding. Still, we were never a couple, which at times was great and sometimes wasn't. It was great because there were no restraints; I could do whatever I wanted, talk to other guys, like other guys, etc. and not feel bad or feel like I am misleading. Yet not great because there were no boundaries. Literally, it went both ways, and he could do whatever he wanted, and I did not have a good reason to get mad. Part of the reason I think I was also up for this type of relationship was that I knew I was not going to give it up. I also knew that was something he probably did on a regular. So it was a relief to know that we can have a relationship, but physically, I was not the one. I am not sure if this is a healthy way of thinking, but in my mind, it made sense. I brought intellect, heart, unconditional love, and emotional support, but physically, I was not where he needed me to be. Therefore, I thought it was okay for him to go get that void from someone else.

Weird, but I was still a virgin and 100 percent sure I was not giving it up. A part of me also thought many guys, especially him, saw that as a challenge—like, "Yup, she is a virgin, but I will get her to give it up." It may have been just something in my mind, but I had only one way to prove my hypothesis—keep talking to them, but no sex. I believed if all they wanted was sex, they would realize it was too much work and move on. Now if he stuck around, then maybe it might be real. I am not proud of my logic, but it made sense to me. I think that is one of the reasons why I never got into any relationship.

It was too much pressure. I did not want to have sex, and I felt like that was a need for most guys I knew. So I did the next best thing—hang out, date guys, but do not have a title or even a committed relationship, so it is not even something they can ask for or even expect. Sounds perfect, right? I am not sure. For most middle-aged adults, it is difficult to control our emotions, and here I was, learning and trying to cope and control mine all at the same time and at a young age. But it was what it was, an understanding between the both of us. Yet I think it discreetly was saying, "I am not enough for you, so I am allowing you to have other partners in your life to fulfill whatever void I am not able to fill or choose not to fill."

Deep...right? Phew!

I must add that during this time, I was still in contact with my friends from Koreatown. I am forever grateful I was because through my two best friends in Koreatown, I went to several church retreats. The church was always the center of our household, but our church was never big, and after the move from Koreatown, many members slipped. So for me, the youth ministries at my friends' churches were more constant and had a lot more options. I know it sounds terrible, but I felt I would meet my future husband at one of these churches. I mean, it would be the ideal situation, right? I am a goody-two shoes and Korean with super Christian Korean parents. It sounds bound that I would marry a guy from church. Also, church was the only time I saw or interacted with Korean guys. However, I felt different, and I think the Korean guys looked at me different. Yup, I remember being the only girl playing soccer with my dad and all the Korean guys and men. I remember my cocky attitude when I would say out loud, "Yea, I am better than any son my dad could ever ask for." You see, your Halbi always wanted a son but instead had two daughters, so I took the role of trying to prove to him how a daughter is way better. Yea, not the wisest thing to conjure up, but it was true. I did my best to make my parents proud—proud that even without a son, they could feel like they succeeded in raising their daughters. No pressure, right? I guess I bring on my own pressure. Sounds familiar? (Aubrey and Ava, I never want you to feel like you are not enough). I may challenge you because I know your capabilities and potential, but I would never want you to put so much stress on yourself to prove to me that you are the best. God made you perfectly for me. All your talents and abilities are his gifts to you so He can shine His light in you. All His gifts given by Him should give Him glory. "Every good and perfect gift is from above" (James 1:17). You are perfect gifts from God.

I want you to know from the bottom of my heart. I am proud to be your mom. You dancing in the mirror by yourself and writing your own songs at age six and playing make-believe with your Barbie dolls with your sister make me so proud. The smallest of things made me and makes me so proud. I am lucky that God chose me to be your mom. Please, do not put any pressure on yourself to make me proud. Because I already am to the fullest. I just want you to live carefree, knowing you are safe and secured. Knowing you can make the biggest *boo boo* and still I will love you and be proud that you admitted to the mistake and told me. I did not choose that life of living carefree, and instead, I overanalyzed everything I did. It was my nature and my situation that made me that way. I am grateful for who it has led me to be. I think it is in you also to be overanalytical and put pressure on yourself to be the best you. Still, I pray it is never to try to prove anything to your dad or me. I am sorry if I ever unconsciously put that pressure on you to be the best. I just want you to have great experiences that I may have never had and learn from them and be happy.

Back to those church retreats, I absolutely thank God I went to as many as I could. It was probably what solidified my relationship with the Lord. I recall several moments during the retreats where I experienced God's presence and all His love. One particular night, it was special than most nights. I am not sure what sparked it, but I was truly overpowered by the Holy Spirit. I let my guard down, and I praised Him and prayed wholeheartedly. I do not even remember the sermon that night. All I know is I was uncontrollably crying and my BFF who was with me hugged me as I wept. Again I have no idea why, but my heart was speaking for me. At that moment, I remember receiving the gift of praying in tongues and just having "my cup overflow." One of my BFFs at the time from Koreatown had that vision;

I will never forget it. It was a special moment. I honestly believe without those retreats, my connection to Jesus would not have been so strong. I was surrounded by young adults who loved the Lord and were proud of it. I was in this special space where we shared one goal: to get closer to God and accept Him to be a part of our daily life. I am forever indebted to my friends, two in particular, who always invited me to church retreats and to the churches. I love you both and am so lucky to still have you in my life today.

And to everyone who took part in worship and in my spiritual growth, I truly thank you.

I want to share that the *church* is not perfect. It is man-made, and man, who are all sinners, are not perfect. I do not think being an active and consistent churchgoer makes you a "good" Christian. There is more to being a Christian than just attending a church. Yet I know what I valued and got most from physically attending church was community. That community is necessary, and I pray God gives us an amazing physical home church. I grew up in a church, literally. You know that the church Halmoni and Halbi go to is a smaller church, and everyone is like family. I pray God will guide us to a home church that is just the right fit for us. As I believe that reading the Word, watching sermons online and praising Him is all wonderful, but I do know what it means to physically be present and be in a community.

I will also admit; I had a few crushes at the various churches, and I think I held these guys on a pedestal. Although I liked the guys from my school, I liked these guys from church differently. I think I liked them in a way where being a parent would, like he may be a good prospect for a husband one day. I know it's a weird feeling I can't really explain. I think it may have to do with reality, like how my parents, your Halmoni and Halbi, would react if I *dated* a Korean guy from church versus a non-Korean guy from school. I quickly realized the Korean church guys were just like any other guy, and as much as I tried to maybe have a relationship with one of them, it was not in my heart. Eventually, I had to tell one of them that, and it was probably the first time I actually hurt a boy's feelings, but I felt it was the right thing. I did not like him as he liked me. It was not something he did, but I just could not continue to lead him on if I did not feel the same way. Was it because I liked someone else, or was it something else? I will come back to this strong conviction I get because it comes to me in many situations as you will see. We did not end on bad terms, not that I recall. Again I try to have cordial friendships even if it may be awkward in the beginning, but I just do not like having ill feelings for anyone and feel it is the best for both parties.

The church retreats were not only my way to the Lord, but it was also my only connection to Korean peers my age. As you know, I did not have any Korean or even Asian friends in my elementary, middle, or high school (Bellflower). A few of my BFFs were Filipino, which were the closest to it. The church allowed me to be proud of my Christian background. Not that I was ashamed, but not many kids in middle and high school were proudly reading the Bible and talking about how amazing Jesus is and that He died on the cross to wash away your sins so you are forever saved and will one day meet Him in heaven. I feel like I lived in two different worlds—one was my reality of the culture around me and being cool and having fun. The other was more in tune with my spirituality, getting to the depth of my soul and what life was truly about and my purpose in life. It was nice to have both. The best of both worlds, but that is not how it works. The Bible states, "No man can serve two masters. You cannot serve God and mammon" (Matthew 6:24). It is difficult because you want guidance as a young adult, but there are many distractions. I think I had difficulty being my true self because I felt I was being two different people depending on the context, which is not good. I wish I was more brave and bold and was my true self from the jump, but that was not what happened. I can blame the distractions, the environment, my parents, etc. for not being 100 percent committed to living out the life God intended me for at that time, but in the end, the problem was me.

No one is perfect, even in the church. One should never put the pastor or the person who is always at church on a pedestal because in the end, we are all human and sinners. So I quickly learned that although the idea of a "good Christian guy" sounded like what my parents would want me to strive for, I, for some reason, never experienced that. Eventually, I stopped going to my friends' church—one of them moved far away, and the other one drifted away from the church herself, so I did not pursue it either.

There was this other Korean guy that I met through our church. We did not become anything other than friends, but I remember that he was the only guy that actually admired and liked that I played rough or just as hard as all the men and boys did. I went with Halbi and all the other men and boys from our small church to play soccer after service. It was a great way for the men and boys to create relationships and have fellowship outside of church. I was like the only girl except for one other girl who followed her brother and dad because she wanted to play also. She was like a little sister who wanted to learn. I, on the other hand, was out there to prove a point.

I always had this weird thing over me where I wanted to show Halbi that his daughters were better than any son. That sounds so arrogant, I know, but most men, especially Korean men, want a son. I am sure it is a male thing, but since I can remember, I wanted to be that girl that proved girls are just as good or even better than boys, especially when it came to my own father. When I went to play soccer, I played hard—harder than I probably should, but I did not care. I would push, shove, and run as hard as I could. When I would make a guy fall, I would just look down upon them like, "Yup, a girl did that," and kept it pushing. I even boldly said, "I am better than any son my dad could ever have," in front of all the men and boys. It is embarrassing to admit when I look back, but it must have come from somewhere. Maybe this is "my daddy issue" or just my own issue of trying to prove that I am *enough*. I think for a good portion of my life, I was trying to prove to myself and to my dad that I, a daughter, was just as good as having a son. It was not Halbi but a pressure I placed on myself, which took a while to realize.

I put other pressures on myself, such as staying the *perfect student* and making the *right decisions* so that I can make it in the world and prove that Halmoni and Halbi leaving Canada was worth it and was not a complete failure. I wanted to prove I was smart enough, even if it was *just* compared to my peers at my school (remember this one?). I mean, it was pretty deep-rooted, but I can now reflect on it. Of course, it was not always bad because I guess it did motivate me to excel, even though I had gone as far as cheating on a test. Not a big deal because people cheat every day, right? Yeah, but I got caught. Not a great feeling to cheat and then be caught proving your insecurities and then feeling like you are being punished by God for making a bad choice. I felt so ashamed, but I mean, how much pressure was I under that I felt the need to cheat to not just pass but to strive for 100 percent on a silly little test. The silver lining is that people saw that I too was not perfect; my peers saw me as one of them yet, although they were unaware that it was not to just pass the test but that I was striving for perfection, to hold down my reputation. Although that got stripped away from me that day, it was a bit relieving because I felt a burden shift off my shoulders. I felt like, "Yeah, I am Grace, and I am not the smartest, most perfect student. It is okay to not get everything right. It is okay to get caught doing something wrong." Had I not gotten caught that day, maybe things would have altered; only God knows. "For I know the plans I have for you, declares the Lord, plans to prosper you and not to harm you, plans to give you hope and a future" (Jeremiah 29:11).

Well, I am way past that now, thank heavens, but during this time, I met this boy from church.

He was a family member visiting, and I got to know him for a short time. I have had some encounters with a few Korean guys, but this one was different. I can tell we did have a connection; I honestly felt like I was in a Korean drama because I could tell he was intrigued by me, and I was a bit interested too. We were never alone or confessed any feelings, but we felt it, and we acknowledged it in other ways, our actions. I was like, "Wow, finally, someone on my level." The only thing was I felt a connection, but it was not a "let's be boyfriend and girlfriend" connection. It was weird. I did not want to hurt his feelings or even try to go down that road, but we never had to. It was almost as if he got it. It is so hard to describe. I almost felt like I was in a beautifully written Korean drama. All these deep emotions but nothing physical and just the deepest of love and self-sacrifice. I know there were feelings from both ends, but all I know is mine was not the kind where I wanted to pursue a relationship. It was just a really good feeling to know that someone recognized me for me and admired it. He knew I was a bit pompous and fierce, yet loving and protective. I felt like he got to know me in a short time and still liked me, my flaws and all. But all that ended when he returned home, and although we tried to keep in touch, it did not work out. We also had a slight language barrier. I was more comfortable in English, and he was more comfortable in Korean.

It is a bit embarrassing to not be comfortable in "my native tongue," but I was never taught Korean, and I did not pursue it or try especially during this time. I was probably more ashamed, especially when I was with my non-Korean friends. It is disappointing to say, but you have to understand, when I was growing up, other cultures would make degrading sounds to mock the various Asian languages, so I did not want to speak it because I did not want to be made fun of. Sadly, at times, I literally was trying to not be Korean.

Anyhoo, back to the guy. We slowly ended our friendship with no hard feelings. I always try to end on a good note because at the end of the day, even if they hurt me really badly and at the moment I despise that person and want to forget every thought of that person, I do not ever want to hold grudges. I want us to be able to one day bump into each other and smile and have a conversation without any hurt feelings. I want the person to learn from their mistakes as I have learned from mine and moved on for the better.

There are several other memories with guys I must have liked, but they are such faint memories, not because they were bad memories but because for whatever reason, I do not remember, or that it left neither a good, nor a bad feeling. I may not remember many of the details of an incident. Still, I think I remember some of the feelings I felt from the experience. I know I kept some of these feelings in a locked journal, but I threw it out after high school. Sadly, I think I was embarrassed, but I wish I had kept them all as I look back. It would have been nice to relive those memories and understand what I felt. I remember the girls at a neighbor's house having a wrestling match with a few guys during a birthday party. I had grass stains and sweat all over. It was fun. Now that I think about it, I wonder if my random drive for wrestling around and literally trying to pin a guy down came from that. Weird. I had forgotten all of that until this moment which has forced me to think about it.

As you know, emotions and feelings come with actions, and I am well aware that you girls will experience different physical encounters. I would not stop you, but as a mother writing this to you, I want you to know that I do not ever want you to just act due to pressure or impulse. I am not saying do not live in the moment as I want you to live life to the fullest and have carefree fun. I just want you to know first that there are no take-backs in life. I want you to know your body is a temple, and it is not yours but God's. "He is the owner, and you are currently the manager," as Pastor Michael Todd would say. I want you to know that just because everyone else is doing a specific activity, it does not mean it is right for you. I want you to know that yes, it may feel good at the moment, but afterward, it can also feel gross and degrading way longer.

I was blessed with wonderful guys in my life who took *no* as a *no* when it came to sex, that I never felt pressured. However, there are other times and other things that I may have allowed to happen that I know were not the best decisions. I know because I remember thinking and feeling a little gross. I obviously had a choice, and for whatever reason, I took part, maybe trying to be cool or thinking it is not a big deal. If you're looking to your feelings for instructions, you are headed for destruction. Trust me. You cannot rely solely on flesh, *how you feel*. How you feel at the moment is not stable. I have learned that feelings change moment to moment. However, the conviction, that inner voice, the Holy Spirit, will show you every time, but it is up to you whether you will listen. I am not saying I was ever pressured or wish I could take some things back. Nope, I cannot because I honestly do not remember, probably because I erased it from my mind from shame or that it has been so long ago that I have forgotten. Yet a woman never forgets. You never quite forget feeling unclean or dirty. Not that it is wrong to show physical affection when you love someone, but I am talking about being part of a physical act with no love in it and just straight pheromones. I know I must have had incidents where it may not have been something I physically wanted to do. Still, because of my emotions or just natural physical reactions, I thought it made sense or vice versa. I may not have loved the person or had any emotional connection, yet physically, I wanted something. Like the infamous R & B singer said, "My mind is telling me no, but my body is telling me yes." I do not agree because I see something wrong with a little bump and grind if your mind tells you no, even if your body is telling you yes. I mean, it may be why the singer is in trouble now, but that's a whole other story. I just want you to know that it is not worth a few seconds or minutes of instant gratification and *feeling good* to feel ashamed and gross for life. You cannot wash off that sort of dirt. Jesus will forgive your sins, yes, but truly coming to repent of your sins and healing can take years of heartache, shame, and pain. I just do not want you to have regrets that may last days or years just because you wanted to feel instant physical gratification of *emotions* or straight pheromones.

I mention this because I am certain you will experience many feelings from various people, and I want you to know every feeling is important. I want you to embrace it, and if you feel it is worth it, talk about it and write it down.

## My "first love"

I know, are we still in that conversation of my "first love"? Of course. It began almost secretly, like we did not want to admit it to everyone else because we sure did not show much in front of people at school. Or maybe it was about our reputation—he was the hot jock every girl wanted to hit or he already had hit. And I was a nerdy, yet athletic, goody-two shoes, who was a virgin and not trying to give it up. I know, it sounds so cliché. I hate it, but trust me, girls, the ending is not what the cliché movies have, so listen up. It is weird, but I guess we both had a reputation to hold up. However, some people knew there was something. I remember cheering for him at football games, making signs and goodies before and after games. I remember hanging out and having real heart-to-heart moments. I remember we slowly became vulnerable and really liked one another. I also remember seeing him with other girls and hearing rumors, some of which I am sure were true. I would think, *Wow, he is very different when alone with me and when in front of others.* But for some reason, it did not really bother me. I mean, yes, it hurt sometimes, but I knew I had something that none of them had with him—a bond and connection deeper than the outside world could see. This connection grew deeper, and I was one phone call or text away whenever he needed me. It was not reciprocated fully, but I was okay with it, or was I? Maybe I was not. Still, since there were no obligations or expectations, I could not be angry. However, I was very fortunate to have such great girlfriends who were in relationships most of high school. I listened to them and their feedback, although I never really asked for advice about Titus, even when he was the only thing I could not resolve. Why? One, my situation was so different from theirs; I did not have a boyfriend. And two, I was not sure if they would really understand. So I confided in my favorite coaches.

I will be honest; at times, I did envy *couples* in high school. I put quotes because, first off, they are high school relationships, and I probably imagined rom-com relationships. Secondly, you just do not know what is truly going on in a relationship. It can all be a facade. I mean, it looked appealing—the holding hands, walking one another to class, celebrating anniversaries, etc. I did want to experience that ideal *high school first love.* A part of me, at the time, wanted that ideal first boyfriend who swept her off her feet and was sweet, romantic, understanding, and only saw her in a room full of many other options. Yet another part of me knew it did not exist; it just was not possible. No boy at age sixteen understands his own emotions and certainly does not know how to treat a girl with just as crazy feelings and thoughts. I know, right? No wonder I was in that predicament. I call myself a realist. I dreamed, but I was held grounded by reality. I think that was the way I was brought up, or maybe it was just me.

Anyway, I don't really remember how or why that happened, but our girls' basketball coaches, ironically, were some of the football coaches. Yup, so most of the guys us girls liked or were dating, our coaches knew the guys personally. Perfect, right? They were our middlemen and men that we trusted and looked up to as a father and big brother. So it was not long when they found out about my situation. What I loved most was they never judged me. I was a Korean girl, raised by typical Korean Christian immigrant parents from Canada, who couldn't confide in my own parents and did not have an older brother or cousin living nearby, so all I had were my coaches. I mean, my parents are wonderful Christian people but also 100 percent old-school. I couldn't tell them about me liking some random African American guy at school. Nope, not me. I had to put on a front like I was all about school, no boys, and definitely not struggling on the inside. I do not remember when this happened, but most of my friends liked African American/Black males. It sounds like it should not be a big deal, and trust me, it was not to us, but looking back, it probably was.

Although this felt normal for us, race/ethnicity was a big part of our culture, but not negatively. Interracial dating was not looked down upon; we actually did not even call it that. It was a beautiful thing to see various races intermingling with no hatred or judgment. I was more worried about my parents and what they would think. Although when it was brought up, I initially blamed them for moving out of Koreatown where there were plenty of Korean males to a city where there were none. However, once it became a real thing, like I really began to not see *color* and started to love and respect the young men I got to know, I became very defensive. Anytime anyone ever questioned why I *dated* African American/Black guys, I would jump the gun and full-on go hard. I would defend them in every way. I look back and think that was great, but I hope I did not actually hurt anyone's feelings. I now realize there is a way to honor and defend a person without putting the other side down, and I hope I was smart enough to do that at the time. However, I probably did not. Knowing my fiery mouth, sometimes I can do more wrong than right when I get very passionate about a topic. Again, emotions can take over rather than speaking love and truth. I am still learning to tame my tongue. I know I have told you; your mouth, your words are powerful and can speak life or death. "The tongue has the power of life and death" (Proverbs 18:21).

The bottom line is that I hope I got across to people who questioned me that I do not choose the one I like or the one I want to get to know by the color of their skin or ancestry line but solely on what

I like and want at the moment. Yes, the physical attraction must be present, but that is not determined by the color of a person's skin but the energy I get when I am near the person and the vibe I sense when we make eye contact. What then holds my interest is the intellectual conversation they can sustain with me. At the age of fifteen/sixteen, that is probably hard to express to people with a totally different view and who just think you like "Black guys because it is a fad." It is probably my own fault for trying to take on this idea that I can show and change people's minds because in the end, we are all God's children.

Thank goodness my coaches listened and helped the best they could. I honestly grew to appreciate them because these African American/Black men became great influences in my life in sports and in relationships. And for that, I am grateful to them. They showed me how guys that age thought and how much more mature a young lady's mind and emotions are without breaking any *guy codes*, which on their behalf did not count because like I said, they were looking out for their basketball girls, who I want to believe were like their own daughters. I also want to give a huge shout-out to them for my mentality, which they helped groom.

I will be completely honest; I had no skills. Halmoni and Halbi were in no position to put me in sports or other extracurricular activities early on, so I had no early training aside from what the public schools offered. My yearning to work hard to get better was always in me. I would literally push myself; I could not dribble through people or shoot threes, but I hustled and showed heart. My dedication and motivation pulled through, and that's how I got my minutes in my games. My resilience of getting back up no matter how much I failed and my grit never allowed me to give up but to try harder. It was weird; I actually was more motivated when they would try to push us to our limits. My coaches not only challenged our physical state but our mental state as well. I loved it because I knew it would make me stronger, especially the suicides when you are dead tired; they were ruthless and would continue to have us run under a specific time frame.

However, if I saw a teammate struggling, I did not mind running extra just so that person knew they're not in it by themselves. Indirectly, as my coaches tested me physically, I think I grew mentally and slowly but, surely, emotionally. As you know, I played volleyball, basketball, soccer, and even ran track for a year. I did not continue with track because it honestly gave me the worst anxiety, just setting myself on the blocks getting ready to take off. I quickly learned that I was a team sports player early on, which explained my mentality and how I took each game. I know some people love that adrenaline kick before coming out the blocks, but for me, it was the feeling in my stomach like right before the roller coaster would drop, and I hated it. Although I was not bad at it, I did not pursue track after my freshman year because of the anxiety—anxiety I probably put on myself. I now realize a lot of the pressure, anxiety, frustrations are thoughts and ideas that were made up in my mind. God did not produce those characteristics in us, but in hindsight, they were made by me because I thought I could do something by myself and either felt insufficient or wanted to give myself props but, in the end, realized I failed expectations. I tried my best to instill in you to "not be anxious about anything, but in every situation, by prayer and petition, with thanksgiving, present your requests to God. And the peace of God, which transcends all understanding, will guard your hearts and your minds in Christ Jesus" (Philippians 4:6–7).

However, I remember walking at like 7:00 p.m. from school after a basketball game we lost—a loss I took to heart. I hated losing. I would literally not talk to anyone and slip away to walk home alone and cry it all out before making it home so my parents would not see. I remember my coach rolling up on me and telling me to get in the car, and I was stubborn, saying, "No, thank you." I knew he wanted me to be safe, but he also respected that I needed my time to cool down. I learned that although losses suck, I grew up the most in those moments. You seem to self-reflect and flourish more after losses because when you are winning, you do not think there is improvement needed. I just want you to know I was lucky, lucky to have great mentorship and wonderful people in my life who I can confide in and talk to, even if it was just losing a basketball game.

I also appreciated talking about the other big thing—boys. Yup, I remember hearing a football coach, not the ones that knew me, tell Titus not to have sex before games after seeing him walking with me. I was embarrassed, abhorred, and wanted to disappear. I remember trying to say it as loud as possible, "We are not having sex!" I did not say it directly to that coach, but I remember telling my other coaches how upset I was. However, they brought me down and leveled with me. These coaches had such a great impact on my life that I was fortunate enough to keep in touch with them even after high school. I know it may sound a little weird to some people as there have been cases where students and faculty had unethical relationships, as those are real. Still, I can honestly say that what we had were genuinely good bonds that all meant well by the grace of God.

I pray you will know what to do in awkward situations. I remember many girls and boys, even myself, having at least one crush on a teacher or faculty member. There was one coach I thought was super hot, handsome, and very nice. I literally remember a conversation we had that I probably wished meant more than it really was because he was such an awesome man. However, I knew he was just being very sweet and nice, and I probably took it to a whole other level. It appeared to be a flirtatious conversation, but I chose not to take it that way but as him being nice. What I took from that, however, was how just simple conversations can be taken out of context and how easily a line can be crossed. Staff, coaches, and teachers have an obligation to always do what is in the best interest of the student; however, we are all human and make mistakes. There are too many real-life scenarios of how one person can take advantage of another or cross a blurred line. I bring this up not to scare you but to make you aware. Adults are not always right, and not all can be trusted. Now that I work in education with students and as a mother, I pray that not only would you have self-control, but so would others around you. We all sin, but I pray that deeply rooted in your heart is Jesus. I realized I cannot protect you from anything. Still, I can help build a strong foundation in your faith in Jesus and believe the Holy Spirit will always be there to protect you and guide you, if you choose to listen. If you listen to the Holy Spirit inside you, you will build pure relationships with all who will be positive influences and who will play a part in navigating your journey through high school and possibly your entire life.

This is a special shout-out to one of my coaches who also passed during the COVID pandemic. Unfortunately, I could not see him during his last few years of life or attend his funeral or memorial. So I would like to take a few lines to just simply share:

> Coach Palmar! No words can express my gratitude, from pushing us to run suicides in the gym and writing up plays to showing me that fried chicken spot and helping me not get played. Your words of wisdom will always be with me. I appreciate you taking your time to express that this little Asian girl is valuable and special. I am so sorry I could not give back what you gave to me, but trust me, I will pass it along to my daughters and to whoever needs it. Just know you have impacted my life and so many others in ways you may never even imagine. I know you're chilling in heaven, bobbin' your head to your favorite music with your shades on. I'mma end with my two favorite lines from you—"You can take the boy out the hood, but you can't take the hood out the boy." "YOLO...but I want to live long." We love you! We thank you! Your legacy will live within us!

I was very lucky to have such influential adults in my life. What I lacked in guidance from immediate family members, I sought out in them. I know I also prayed but I think community and physically talking it out to a therapist would have been very beneficial. A lot of the times you can answer your own questions or find out the solution to the issue just by venting and saying it out loud. Boy, did I need it with my situation. Although I did not have a licensed therapist, I was able to be 100 percent real and transparent with my coaches. I did not hold back how I felt and what I thought. Neither did my coaches. Yet, they did not judge me or make me feel like I was making a bad or not so smart decision, but they made me think twice and reconsider before I acted upon my emotions. Like I said, Titus was a pretty well-known fella on our school grounds, and a hot commodity amongst females, it appeared. He had a reputation, and because I was around him, I also fell into a category. (Be careful who you surround yourself with). So annoying, yet in most cases, it holds true. You usually are in cliques, playing the same sport, or sharing the same interests. To me, it was another perk that our relationship was sort of on the low. I did not care for the publicity or everything else it came with, so I think I started to distance myself. I mean, it was not that hard. I still liked him, but I made sure not to grow stronger feelings. The odd thing about feelings, especially at that age, is that you really cannot control your emotions or feelings. To be honest, I do not remember specific details, probably because I tried very hard to totally erase all memories we had and the feelings he gave me, good and bad. But I know that I must have really cared for him as one of my BFFs knows we would cry, I mean bawl our eyes out, in my car about our situations about the guys we truly cared for. I mean, we got it bad; Usher was right 100 percent. These love songs must have come from somewhere, and we were bawling our eyes out, listening to sad love songs and talking about every detail of these boys. We often would write a text and erase it or start to call and hang up; we were both going through it. We were going through different situations yet the common denominator was heartache. I was in a lingo of wanting to stop the "relationship" we had, but yet it was awkwardly so hard to let go. It did not make sense. I had common sense, and nothing about our "relationship" made any sense. Yet, I would try to say goodbye and discontinue our discreet relationship but something always reeled me back in. He never forced me to stay or even fought it when I would give signs that I was over it. He did not have to because he knew he got me. There came a time where I gave in so many times even when I would bluntly say I'm done. He knew in his heart it wasn't and confidently let me have the space I needed. Yet, he was always there with open arms when I came back.

Looking back, I do not necessarily think the boys we were crying over actually meant any harm. They were not malicious, nor wanted to hurt us intentionally. I think they just wanted to live life and keep us near like a security blanket. To be fair, he did nothing wrong. We were not "together," so he was never "cheating." I was just dealing with the emotions I had and trying to figure out the unusual relationship. By my junior year, he was away at a division one university on a scholarship, exploring and experiencing everything. You would think perfect. He is physically gone so I can move on and forget him. Girl, I still wanted him, apparently. I wanted him, but yet I wanted to let go all at the same time. I wanted him at moments, but at the same time, I did not want him because I knew it was not right. This type of relationship could not be heaven-sent. At the time, I did not know what it was, but now I know it was the Holy Spirit assuring me that he was not my husband to be, and this was just an experience. Just a note, even though you know the Holy Spirit is speaking to you and showing you all the signs, you are still not going to see it if you are not ready. I say that because I realized that the quiet voice I would hear my entire life was the Holy Spirit in me, but I only listened and obeyed when I truly surrendered and was ready to hear it. I did not know it then, but it was strong enough to veer my steering wheel when I was going off-road but soft enough to allow me to make my own decisions. I know it's crazy, but God had my back from day one. I also prayed.

When I got weary and confused, I prayed. Thank heavens.

I do not remember exact timelines, but I know he came in and out of the picture several times throughout my life. For a long time, I would just make sure he knew I was there no matter what. Like no matter what he did, I was that constant support and love. Maybe I was placed in his life at that time to be his constant in his forever-changing lifestyle. Maybe we were both helping one another without really knowing we were. I could not imagine just packing all my things, leaving to a whole new state, and just expected to thrive educationally and physically on and off the field. Mentally and emotionally, he may have needed our relationship more than he and I may ever know.

Maybe God placed me in his life at that moment for a reason. Maybe what we had was bigger than just emotions. Maybe? Who knows? Or maybe I liked that when he came to visit because I felt like we were both in our own world and escapade. And for that night, we can pretend we were meant to be together. We would bring out stressors and burdens and put it aside and just for that time together we were in complete bliss. It was not shared or spoken, but it was a moment we both needed and was able to share companionship, understanding, and best of all with no judgment. Not many people knew about it because we both knew it was something between us, and we did not care or feel that it needed to be accepted or known by others. We had no titles and rules; we just enjoyed one another's company and had a real connection. I also wanted to be the one constant he can count on. What a weird thing to do, right? I would still live my life and do my own thing—date, which in my mind and definition at the time was getting to know other guys and hanging out with other guys I might have had some feelings for. Still, at the end of the day, if he needed to talk or hang out, I was there. I found out my love for him was this weird unconditional love. I did not need to know every day that he cared or loved me. All I wanted to do was let him know and give him no doubt that I cared and loved him no matter what. I gave him all the assurance he needed to conquer the world ahead. I did not care to hold onto him anymore; I just wanted him to succeed and do well, knowing that someone believed in him and cared for his well-being.

I am not sure what exactly sparked my emotional growth, but I know my emotions became more matured as I was able to control them and verbalize them. I began to see our relationship for what it was. I realized that you cannot hold onto someone or the fantasy of what could be because the more you hold on, the more they slip away or realize it isn't real. So all you can do is love them so they know you won't slip away and just cherish what you had. Does this love sound familiar? Now that I look back, I feel like this love is the kind of love you have for your child or a small glimpse of how God loves us. I think this is how I am with most of my relationships; not sure if it is good or bad, but it is just how I have come to deal with relationships all around. I try to always assure the other person that I am always here for them and will always love them even if they are not there for me and do not feel the same way. It is a weird trait that I have always had. For a long time, I thought that was how everyone worked, but through heartbreaks from all walks of life (relationships with friends, boys, family, etc.), I realized you cannot expect to get back what you give to others. You must give to give and not to receive anything back. I think that is one of the biggest lessons I learned about relationships. Everyone has different ideas about relationships and love. I decided to give the best version of what I thought was love and a relationship, and if it is reciprocated, then awesome. If it is given back in a different way, cool, and if it is not acknowledged, that is also okay because I gave what I wanted to give in its entirety.

As a mother now, I can honestly say no matter what you girls do in life, I will always love you and believe that you can do anything, God willing. I do not need to hear you say "I love you" or even show me that you love me because I would still love you with all I have. Phew! Dang, I feel like the Holy Spirit yelling. Saying that is God. God is love. He gives and loves no matter what.

You can drift off, but He keeps you anchored and will not let you go far. Trust me! Crazy!

Also, I know you are probably thinking, *How did you date other guys when you felt so strongly for Titus?* Well, my dear, that is what I want to point out. At this age, and I think until you choose to be with *the one*, but especially at this age, it is totally normal to like more than one person at the same time. Not in a "player" like way but because we are young and learning about ourselves, and hormonal changes do not help. I am sure there were plenty of young kids my age who liked more than one person, even if they had a *boyfriend* or *girlfriend*. I am 100 percent sure because I know many folks who were in relationships and questioned themselves, especially when they find out another person likes them. They would ask themselves, "Is this person really *the one* for me?" "How do I know he/she is my soulmate if I have not explored or been with other people?" I think those questions are natural to have. I was never in that predicament myself because I was never in a committed relationship at a young age, but I think it is human nature. You got something but may want something you just cannot have. I do not know exactly what causes this phenomenon, but what I do know is how this causes chaos. Chaos to a young preteen/teen is possibly lying and cheating. I never cheated or lied, at least not that I remember. I always tried to stay true, especially to the guys I was talking to. I mean we were all in the same school. It was not like I was talking to other guys from different area codes (I was not that confident yet). So I knew it would get around, and I would hate to look like a fool or, worse, a liar. I always kept it real. The only thing I did not keep real was probably the relationship and how I felt about Titus. Do not get me wrong, I did like other guys and dated and never felt obligated. However, I never actually told anyone I was still in contact with Titus. One, because we were not together, so really there was no reason to. Two, because he was so inconsistent; I honestly never knew when he would pop up unless it was a break or a holiday. Even then, he may not hit me up, so it was always up in the air. But I shared a connection with Titus that I never really felt with any other guy in high school. He, for some reason, made me feel safe.

When we would just lay in silence, I would literally wish I could just stop time and be in that moment a little longer before going back to reality. It was a feeling I did not feel with any other guy I dated in high school. I have no idea why, but I think that is the only fond, true memory I have of him during high school. Everything else I tried to forget and eradicate from my brain.

Just for the sake of trying my best to open up to you and try to share with you my most vulnerable yet heartbreaking memories, I tried. I really did. I even watched movies about high school, drove past where we would walk together many times, but nothing. I will say this though; he was my first "love," my first "heartbreak," the first guy that ever made me feel beautiful in my own skin and body. I do remember him looking at me after I say or do something very random, and the look he gave me made me feel adored, and then he would say how "cute" I was or just how "bomb" my body was. I know a boy should not give you validation; you should already have it. Yet that is not how it happened. My first boost of confidence came from myself, but his validation probably made me feel some type of way. I mean, let's go back. I am 100 percent Korean. I was one of very few Asian girls at my school. I had the typical sleek black hair, slanted eyes, and a noncurvaceous body type. I was not one of the top most attractive girls from the jump. It took a while to grow into loving myself. However, what I lacked in curves and looks, I knew I had an abundance in heart and soul. So yes, he made me feel beautiful physically, but I knew what I had was more than meets the eyes. I knew I touched souls and can make hearts flip. Talk about confidence, or is that arrogance?

He was also the same boy who put me through the worst pain without even knowing it. I say he probably did not know it because for some reason we (female and male) seem to think we can read one another's mind. I probably never truly opened up and explained how he would make me feel. I think I never told him because I already felt vulnerable because I was feeling those feelings and was simply embarrassed to put myself out there. Or I assumed he would magically know. Looking back, I should have told him. It would have maybe made him better understand my perspective. However, another reason why I probably did not want to tell him all my feelings and thoughts and totally put myself out there is because I did not completely trust him. It changed later down the road (next book), but at this point, we were in high school and not in a "real" relationship. It was difficult to just say, "Hey, here is my entire heart." Also, it did not help that sometimes I felt I was a conquest that he was trying to conquer because he conquered everyone else, as if I was hard to get, and he stayed because I was a challenge. Then of course, he would look me in the eye and say, "You are it," and then confusion all over. Nonetheless, he was also the one that throughout my young adult life, put me on *game*. He did not lay out the game and show me what each piece did. Nope, he just played the game, and I was one of the pieces in it, and I had to either win or lose. At least that's how I felt at the time, and now looking back, it is the only way to really understand the game and perfect it. The only thing different about this game is that there is really no right or wrong but just different scenarios one would be in depending on the actions one takes. It adapts as you change directions and evolve as a person/ character in the game. Just experiencing the emotions he placed me in or, rather, that I placed myself in, taught me a lot about myself and this game called love. I learned how the brain of a guy kind of works. I learned that I needed to, above all, control my emotions, feelings, and all actions. Self-control is definitely mentioned in the Bible, and I can now 100 percent believe that is key. If I could tell my younger self the Bible has all the answers, I still would not believe it; as an older adult, I not only believe it, but I live it.

You are probably wondering how, where, and when did we hang out. I know, it sounds insane, especially now that I have daughters myself, but Halmoni and Halbi trusted me, and yes, I would be out late. They would call wondering where I am. I was never able to fully tell them exactly where I was but with a friend or friends. I want you to know I would much rather you hang out together in my house and tell me the truth about your whereabouts than lie and get hurt or worse. I know God had his hands on me throughout these times because the Lord knows I was not always telling the entire truth. However, the flip side was I did not do anything that involved breaking the law or putting myself or anyone in danger. Still, yes, I have been in a room with a boy at night, alone, which I am not condoning at all. But again, I am trying to be as transparent as I can so that you will not be afraid to tell me the truth. I am so grateful that Halmoni and Halbi gave me my freedom. I know many peers that would sneak and lie just to do what they wanted in the end. However, the only downfall of putting yourself in situations that you think are best for you but may not be is that there may be activities that will be present that are also not the best for you. You may think, "I got this. I can control myself," but in the end, we are all human and succumb to sin. I mean, come on; Eve was persuaded by a reptile to eat an apple from the one tree God said no to. Why did she even go near that tree and place herself in that predicament? All I am saying is, emotions, peer pressure, hormones, pheromones will get the best of you. It is definite. Therefore, as parents, I now see it is just best to not even place a young adult in those predicaments. Well, I am guilty. I placed myself in many situations knowing what can happen. I would always tell myself I do *love* him, and we are not having *sex*. Yet that was the wrong mentality. First of all, sin is sin. No one sin is better than the other. Secondly, *love*? Again, it was love to me at that age, and I knew I was not ready to have sex for many reasons, but I also realized doing anything physical leaves a stain. A stain meaning it is a physical interaction, and I should not have taken it so lightly as it does stay with you. I will admit he was the first person that I shared more than just a kiss. I do not regret my actions, but I want to share that I should not have justified it by thinking it was a "not so bad" sin. I know I was one that was not experienced and in many cases, at school, being "experienced" is cool. I pray that you know the difference between what is considered *cool* in the eyes of flesh versus in God's eyes. May you yearn for God's will. I pray you will seek God and know that even if you feel alone and no one understands you, God is there. I pray you will wait and be exposed to these things later in life, but I also know God's plans are greater. I know many of the situations I was in helped me mature; especially during this relationship, I grew up emotionally. As much as I want to shield you, I know you will do the right thing. I also know you will do what you want at the end of the day, no matter what your dad or I say. I can only tell you what I learned from what I did and pray. I will also bring the Word as the Word is God, and I am telling you "the Bible is the only book that, as you read it, it reads you," as Pastor Michael Todd would say. Lastly, you may hide it from me or your dad, but you cannot hide anything from God which in turn will convict you.

## My love language

My love language was not the norm. I didn't show public affection or verbally say "I love you." I showed my love through acts of service or just actions. I was a huge believer that actions speak louder than words. I also think that my roots came from the Bible (1 John 3:18) and from being raised by my parents as that was their love language. Plus those Korean dramas definitely hit home. I remember watching them and feeling and seeing how the characters wouldn't just go off and have physical interactions. Nope, their acts of sacrifices, actions and reactions expressed the depth of love they had for one another. I understood and knew that that was *love*—putting the person you love before your own needs and wants. So I did that all the time. The only bad part was my way of love was beyond what *love* should be in high school.

Although I do not regret giving and showing love in the only way I knew, I say it is my fault because in high school, you do not know each person's love language and what is compatible, nor do you talk about it. Hence, it was naive to expect Titus to understand my *love* and *love* me back the way I wanted. Most teenagers at this age think love is this one thing that is universal when in actuality, love is so different from one person to the other. Girls, I want you to know that love to you is so different from love to the next person, and your expectations of it will also be totally different. And that, my dear, can hurt one or both of you.

I learned my love needed to change and be on the high school level, not the deep, true love stuff. Truth be told, when you are in high school, it is easy to be distracted by boys, relationships because that is all you see around you and in the media. But, girls, there is an entire world out there. Ask yourself, is this guy you *love* really the love of your life, the one you will be with forever when you haven't even seen or experienced anything beyond the gates of your high school? I sound pessimistic, but it is how I would want you to think because about 80 percent of me felt this way. Somehow, I quickly got the epiphany that I was not going to meet my husband at sixteen. I don't know why I was thinking about meeting my *true love/husband* at this age. I blame the fairy-tale love stories that were embedded in our brains—meeting Prince Charming in a magical way and living happily ever after and the societal norms that have brainwashed us. That's not reality. Reality is that you are young and changing physiologically and physically. And so are the boys; they are going through it emotionally and physically just as you are. Of course, I have no firsthand experience of being a boy, but I know they are human, and love songs are not all written by females. Actually, I think the really good ones are mostly by males, and we females love them so much because we are getting a glimpse of how they feel, which is exactly what we feel. "Men are from Mars, and women are from Venus"—we are very different, but we have so much more in common.

# PART 4

# Lessons through the Game

## *The epiphany*

Statistically, I would reason with myself (and I hope you do too) that most people who are together in high school do not last. I think I only know one person who is still with the person they met in middle or high school. Yes, that one person is one of your aunties. I am proud to say I helped make that happen in a very minute way, but I know it was difficult for them to grow together, go through trials, and question themselves, is this person really the one for me? You girls can ask them about their love story one day, but all I know is that it is rare. I am not saying it cannot happen to you, but what I am saying is don't count on that. I sound like a terrible mother, stopping you from experiencing love, but that is not what I am trying to do. I honestly hope you experience *love* in all stages of your life, especially in high school, because I think that is probably going to be the most innocent and purest form of *love*, innocent because it will probably be your first and pure because it will be what *love* means to you.

I was 80 percent practical and realistic and knew that I would not meet *the one* yet. However, of course, I had the other 20 percent that still believed or hoped for the fairy tale, like in the rom-com movies where you meet the love of your life in high school and live happily ever after. But like I said, I was practical. I knew in my heart that 80 percent was real, and 20 percent was fantasy. And my life, well, it was too real to suddenly become a fantasy…or so I thought. On one of my many tear-filled nights, it hit me; he ain't the one. Christina Aguilera said, "Let it go, and if it comes back, it's yours. That's how you know it's for keeps. Yeah, it's for sure." It made sense to me at that time, and I did my best to let it go. Just like Elsa, "Let it go!" I mean, really, how hard could it be? He ain't even the one, so why are you tripping? I felt like the Holy Spirit was yelling by this point. But to get to this point, it took a minute—longest minute ever.

But, honey, after I decided that, I had the time of my life—no attachment and no commitment to no guy. I would go out and hang out with whoever I wanted and have fun. I remember parties—no, not in mansions or on the coast overseeing the beach—literally, random house parties, or we would all go to this clublike room at one of the parks with a DJ and dark lights. Let's just say we would come out with sweat dripping down and our booties all blue. They were blue because when you are wearing light-colored pants and dancing/grinding on one another while sweating, the blue from the jeans would rub onto them. Yes, we drank alcohol (not something I am proud of). But we were somewhat responsible as it was usually at one of our friend's houses, and I would spend the night, and we had our Momma Tita who would be there watching us. It was amazing to have a parent who understood us, and rather than us having to sneak around, she let us do what we were going to do anyways but in the safe haven of her house and with her present—nothing out of control, but trust me; once you are in high school, you may start to become a bit rebellious. Special thanks to Tita! Those that know her understand that she was all of our mommas when we felt like our own would not understand. Thank you for being that Mom!

I just want you guys to be honest with me because, yes, it is fun in high school, and you think it just makes you feel great, but many things can go wrong. Without lecturing you, I just want you to know I was so lucky. I honestly know God was always with me because I will be one hundred with you; I am sure if I was with the wrong people and drinking alcohol, many not-so-good things could have happened, but I thank God for all the wonderful guys and girls I met and got to know who never took advantage of me. I never felt scared or threatened. Even though I was in many situations that could have easily gone down south, the guys took *no* as an answer and respected me even if my body might have been saying otherwise. Nothing bad happened to me. With that said, I do not ever want you to be in that situation where it could have gone the other way. I pray you girls will meet strong and good girlfriends and boyfriends throughout your life, especially in high school. I mean, we can try our best to put you in the *best* schools, the *best* environment, and even the *best* scenarios.

Still, I don't think it's the schools or the place because there are douchebags and wonderful young men and women at every school and city. What I do know is that I can only put my trust in God and build a solid foundation in your heart to know what is right for you and what is not. First Corinthians 6:18 says, "Flee from sexual immorality. Every other sin a person commits is outside the body. But the sexually immoral person sins against his own body." I wish I had the self-control to run.

I am terrible with my timeline, but I am trying my best to keep it somewhat of chronological and sequential order. Still, I cannot guarantee I am right. However, everything I am telling you about my perspective and emotions was real, and I can guarantee that.

When I turned fifteen and a half, I got my driver's license to relieve Halbi from having to drive us to the market and running errands for my mom after he got off work. I also got a working permit from my high school to legally start working at a real job. I wanted to stop relying on my friend's dad to keep up with a "job," and many of our other friends were now interested in the gig. I mean, it was sweet—no taxes, straight cash. But I wanted to take it into my own hands and find a job. I decided to apply at different places in the mall. This is very typical; not sure how normal this would be when you are this age, but I think most kids my age had their first job at a retail store or the mall. Anyways, I ended up working at the movie theaters which, in hindsight, was the best thing ever, not only for the perks but because of the people I met. I met some of the most wonderful people there.

First is Joe. I honestly hope one day you will meet him. Aside from my coaches, he was the only other male figure that I confided in, and I truly cared about his thoughts. I would introduce him to the guys I liked and later ask what he thought. I would talk to him after I got off and see what he thought about my situation. He was the head security at the movies, and he was like a father/uncle/grandfather and everything, and I looked to get his approval before daring to actually act upon anything. His outlook and responses I took to heart because I am sure he has been there, done that, and I knew he was always looking out for me and had the best interest for me. We are still in contact today, and he will always have a special place in my heart, for he was never judgmental but always loving and helped me become stronger emotionally during some dark times.

Next is Jess. I loved her. She showed me a whole other world. She was like the big sister I never had, and she treated me like a friend and a sister all in one. She also provided a lot of wisdom and love. I did not like the love situation she was in, but I loved how real and open she was about it. She knew who she was and did not care what anyone thought, and I aspired for that. She was also soft and was in love, and I loved how happy that man made her even though I always thought she deserved better and more, but she wanted him and chose him, and I could not argue with that. Again, she knew what she liked, and that was that.

Lastly, my posse. "The boys" were my constant. They were there when my BFFs weren't. Not in a bad way. My ROD BFFs were mostly in relationships and, girls, you'll learn early that once someone is in a relationship, that takes most of their recreational time. If my girls were happy, I was happy. But I had a lot of time to myself which is great, and I loved being alone, but my boys also kept me busy. We would hang out and just have fun. But my fondest and most memorable memories are those late-night runs. I always loved running. I used to go run the bleachers with one of your aunties during summer vacation. We would say it was to get in shape, but I was doing it to relieve my stress and keep me sane. When I run, I ran. I would push myself. It was not to look good or to prove to anyone else. It was for my mental and emotional health. I loved the physical pain of being sore. I think it distracted me from the emotional and mental pain or issues I had at that moment. To this day, I love being sore. I love feeling it in your butt and legs while getting up and sitting down. I love laughing so hard that it hurts my abs because I just did abs. I love all that. I know it's weird, but I loved it, and I loved running because I would rather feel physical pain than be emotionally or psychologically drained. I think this is still embedded with me. I want to apologize for ever taking any stress or anger out on you. I hope you girls understood I needed to exercise to burn all that out. I hope I never made you feel like I chose exercise over spending time with you, but I chose my mental health so that I can come back in thirty minutes and be a better mom to you guys (sidetracked).

I would go running in the middle of the night at Liberty Park (the bleachers were usually locked) to just be by myself and let some steam off. Once the boys knew I was doing this, and I told Joe, they were adamant. I told them every time I went because they knew how dangerous it could be. I mean, honestly, I never thought it was dangerous because I knew Jesus is my protector, and He got me. Also, I was pretty confident in my self-defense skills. But they were right because I would sometimes run the riverbed in the dark with hardly anyone there, and a stranger could have come from behind me, and boom, no one would even notice. Thank God it never happened, but Joe also made the boys always keep me company. They actually loved it because it was also their way to hang out and get fit. So it was perfect. I would go with them, and honestly, I am glad they came because there was never a dull moment, and they made me happy. They made me feel loved and safe. During this time, I learned those feelings you think you can only get from a significant other can actually come from God alone and some good friends and not necessarily from a boy or girl you like. I thank God for this time because I began to see I did not need a boyfriend, and I did not want one.

## BFFs

I hope you girls are fortunate to have and meet strong, loyal, and genuine friends because I learned that people may come and go in your life, but true friends are hard to come by. As you know, I have my BFFs from high school and one from elementary, your aunties. Your aunties and I have been through it all—boyfriend breakups, girlfriend breakups—but we are still standing strong to this day. One of the most memorable things your grandmother told me is, some friends are here for a reason or a season, but then some are there a lifetime. Your aunties are my friends that I know will be here for a lifetime. I have a couple others like them, but I am bringing them up because I spent every day in high school with your aunties. We ditched school, drank underage together, and did some not-so-good things together. We also experienced the highs of high school together—played sports, a part of the Filipino club, and the Associated Student Body. Yup, I was president of ASB, and they were all part of my cabinet. We felt like we ran the school. I hope we never came off cocky or rude to other students, but I can only tell you my perspective. All I know is all of us, by senior year, had confidence like no other. But all the confidence in the world still did not stop the immature feelings we could not give up. So we basically put ourselves through the heart-wrenching experience of *heartbreak*. I am not going to lie; I felt so lucky I had a BFF who was with me through the treacherous pain called heartbreak. We went through it together, and obviously, any experience is always better with a BFF.

Girls and guys are emotional; guys, they just express it differently. For girls, we cry, vent, and write about it. I believe boys take it out physically or shut down and shut out folks. Anyway, if I had a son, I would say, "Don't think it is weird to express yourself, especially to a girl. And don't believe others who would laugh and say it is not cool. They either never experienced having a female they can confide in, or they secretly are and just fronting." Trust me, I know. During the time I was *dating* and getting to know a lot of these "tough" guys, I got to see a glimpse of their *soft side* inside their hearts and emotions. It just takes a while to get them to open up. Many appear to have some layers, but if you sit tight and show you are genuine and would listen, they will feel it and speak from the heart. Listen to love songs; those are feelings written out into songs from experiences, whether about heartbreak or what could have been. Like I said, many of the greatest are written by men.

## Dating/crushes

"I am getting to know you and him and him. I am no one's girlfriend and not doing anything physical with any of you yet. Still, I wanted to let you know before we continue so you can make your decision whether to be a part of it or not." That's the gist of what I was telling the boys. Or so I hoped I was getting across. Everyone has their own perspective or interpretation, so I can only express mine. Sounds a little familiar? It was very similar to the situation I was in and have been with Titus. We knew what we had, and it was our choice to stick around. I know, right?

Balls! I definitely grew some. I guess Titus taught me a thing or two. Titus taught me to be real about my situation and then leave it to the other party to decide if they want to stick around or not. I also learned a lot from seeing things from the outside, and even though I never had a "boyfriend," I had a lot of girlfriends who had them, so I would watch and learn from both sides. I learned about how the guys act and react and how the girls act and react. I ain't gon' lie; there were some amazing guys I got to know. I judged them as not-so-smart boys who only think with their dicks, chasing any girl who was willing to give it up. Yet many had deep thoughts, humor, charm, and were beautiful in each of their own ways. I also loved meeting their families as it tied everything and made me see the person in a whole different light. But in the beginning, I literally had to inform them all that I was a "virgin and keeping it that way." Again, keeping it one hundred and honest from the jump, I made some good friendships and even liked some.

I had an amazing high school experience. I remember *dating/getting to know* a star football player and his amazing family, but for some reason, I did not pursue it. I remember hanging out with another great prospect (sounds terrible like I am looking through resumes, but low-key, I think I was) who was a smart, respectful guy, yet I did not feel the connection. Then there was Micah, and I was definitely smitten. Honestly, I met his older brother first but knew there was no chance for many reasons, but he was such a great guy. I knew if he had a younger brother, it would be perfect, and he did. We were each other's valentine and got each other gifts. He was probably the sweetest guy I have ever met and so different from the other guys I *dated*. First and foremost, he was not a jock! He was soft-spoken and just someone who would never break a girl's heart. Sounds perfect, right? Yea, nope. Again, I didn't pursue it.

There was also Nicholas who told the world and everyone in it how in love he was with me. He was great too, but again I never "committed" with any of them. Sounds crazy even thinking about it. How did I all of a sudden have options but yet wanted no one? I thought it was because I did not feel strongly about the guys, or it faded after it became a possibility. Not sure, but I do remember Titus coming in and out during those times. Yup, he would come to visit, and I would see him either in a group setting or just him and me. I would tell him about it, making him almost boastful. I do not blame him for his pompous attitude. I mean, I told you I would give him assurance that I would always be there for him, and he felt that deep unconditional love from me; it was undeniable. However, he thought just because I cared dearly and always wanted to be there for him, it meant *I was his*. He literally would say, "You are mine." He would say it did not work out with that guy because of him. Not going to lie; a part of me would fall into his charming and arrogant ways, but the funny thing is you are never actually "someone's." You can try your best to make sure that person is "yours" and hold on tight, but you cannot hold onto anything that was never yours in the first place.

In the beginning, I thought he was right. He would somehow pop right back into my life after I was dating someone or right after I stopped liking someone; his timing was impeccable. I would find myself thinking, *Is this God's sign to tell me he is the one or God's sign to tell me that none of them was the one?* Whatever it was, I knew in my heart he was not the one. I mean, he couldn't be, right? Then of course, I was sideswiped by some guys I looked up to as brothers. I have always wanted an older brother. I do not know why, but I envied girls with older brothers, someone who looked after them, protected them, and yet did not see them in any sexual way and did not want anything other than their *sister* to be well and happy. So I gravitated toward older guys who took me under their wing. I realized later on that even those relationships can get a little weird if you ain't blood.

Anyway, there was a particular moment that kind of screwed me up. Since I hung out with Titus when he was down, I hung out with his typical guy friends whom he stayed with. I became part of the little posse, or so I thought. I got so comfortable with a couple of them that I decided we could be friends and hang out even when Titus wasn't there. First, I wanted to prove that I would still be a friend even if Titus was not physically there. And doing so gave me peace of mind since they were like brothers to Titus. I felt they would not cross the line. One day, in daylight, I came and hung out with one of them. We were just talking, and he actually told me, "Don't you want to practice so you can be perfect for him or whoever you end up with?"

Those may not have been the exact words, but I felt like someone punched me in the throat because I was hurt that he was trying to get something out of me, whether it was a reaction or physically. Also, it sucked because I never thought of it that way.

"Nope, I do not want to practice with anyone else except the one I end up with. If I suck, he can help me become better. I will probably think it was amazing no matter how he performs because I have nothing to compare it with" was basically what I said. Again, culture throws out how being "experienced" is a positive attribute. Then I probably felt uncomfortable and left not too soon after. I believe I never hung out with him one-on-one again. I won't lie; I do not think I ever felt 100 percent comfortable with him around, even when Titus was there. I just felt a little disrespected and let down. That experience also made me think, *Wow, do guys really care about the performance of a girl in the bedroom? Geez, sex life is a lot more than I can even imagine.* I was not a girl who watched porn or images, but I felt like it is a pretty self-explanatory thing. I had no idea there were ways of being good and bad. I did not want to have sex. I did not want to lose my virginity, and now I had to worry about whether I am good at it. Wow! In hindsight, it was a good lesson. I have to be less naive and realize who I can truly be vulnerable with. I am sure I probably told Titus, but I mean his BFF did not mean any harm. I never felt threatened. He was honestly one of the coolest guys Titus had as a friend. I am sure Titus was a little bothered but probably figured he was just shooting his shots to see what he can get in. I mean, if you do not shoot any shots, your chance of making any is zero. Guy code? I don't know, but it still hurt. I wanted to believe that there are guys who just want to be my friend without expecting or wanting anything out of it. I started to think that having an "older brother" figure is not what is best for me.

# PART 5

# My First Boyfriend

Then there was Ezekiel. He was in most of my AP classes in my senior year, and he played baseball. Yea, far-fetched, but there was something. I have no idea who liked who first, but all I know is we started to hang out a lot by ourselves, and I was intrigued because I never met a guy like him. I honestly did not even notice him until senior year, but he had been there the entire time. At this time, I had grown very confident and knew what I wanted, or so I thought. He started "courting" me. I put those in quotes because I honestly would never use that term back then, but now that I look back, I would call it that. I mean, he would do some of the sweetest and most romantic things you only hear about or see in movies. I remember I would get ready to go to school, and there would be flowers on my car windshield, or he would literally cook a candlelight dinner at his house and invite me over. He took me on our first date to dinner at Rainforest Cafe in downtown Disney and refused to let me pay or at least go half. He opened doors, pulled out chairs—I mean the whole nine. I am sure there were so much more that I just, unfortunately, do not have it all detailed and memorized. Yet I do remember feeling very special, and like I said, sometimes it felt like a movie. Yet I would dodge him every time he would bring up girlfriend/boyfriend stuff. By now, most people have heard about us, and he started to become a hot commodity. Other girls noticed his charm, wit and, yes, his body because it was rock solid—muscular but not like a crazy bodybuilder and, of course, abs which drove all the girls crazy. I know, right? Sounds cliché. But to me, he was different not because of his physical build but because of his intellect. I got to know the nerdy yet clever and very sarcastic but charming Ezekiel. Before him, I never really went on a date with a guy who opened doors, bought flowers, and paid for me. I think that's called chivalry. It was pretty much dead by the time I was a senior, or I was never introduced to it properly. I have no idea, but I pray it makes a comeback by the time you girls start to date because it makes you feel some type of way. Although I am all about independent women and how we can do for ourselves, it is nice to know you have an individual who will give you their jacket when you are freezing or hold the door when your hands are full. I also think it has a lot to do with our upbringing and circumstances. For instance, I told you we were struggling financially, so I also figured many of the peers were probably in the same boat or a little better or worse. Our parents were not rich, and many had single parents. I actually felt very lucky that one of my best friend's dad would hook us up with under-the-table jobs. Since middle school, we would pass out flyers or be at the farmer's markets for his gym, etc. Anyways, I never asked my parents for money for anything that was a luxury (nice clothes, dresses for dances, my cell phone, etc.) Yup, all God. He provided me with the opportunity to get my first job through Scarlett's dad. I would take care of a lot of the paying when I would go eat or have a smoothie with a guy, and it never bothered me. I actually felt like I was being a confidant and a good friend and never felt used by them—well, most of the time. Anyways, back to Ezekiel, he was chivalry at its best, at least to me, because I was never treated that way. Romantic—I mean, I do not like corny, but it was nice getting flowers randomly and getting surprise dates.

So I planned to surprise him and had my friends help me make a poster. I talked to his baseball coach to get permission to use the visiting side dugout one Friday afternoon. I waited for him in our usual spot, and this time, I walked into the baseball field, and he turned and saw the sign. "Will you be my boyfriend?" I know it totally sounds like a movie. And it felt like it. He said yes, and we kissed. He was so happy, and I was too. I got my movie ending! I told him I was avoiding the subject of becoming a couple because I wanted to ask him. I never asked a boy out before, so I wanted it to be my first and wanted to go all out. So it began. We were a *couple* holding hands, a kiss before class; the ideals I always wanted when having a boyfriend in high school were becoming a reality. We went to Sadie Hawkins together, and my BFFs started to kind of get him. He was different from our norm, but I liked it. He confessed his love to me and started to say "I love you." I was flattered but not quite ready, so I told him, and he was totally understanding. I met his biological father and went to an amazing baseball game held at the Los Angeles Coliseum, which alone was pretty special. His father was amazing, and I felt even closer to him and his heart.

All was well, until one day, he was late to our usual spot. I didn't want to be late to class, so I started to walk off and texted him. Then someone, I honestly do not remember who exactly but a person that would not lie and a good source, told me that they saw Ezekiel kiss one of my friends. I was in disbelief, like "No way" and kind of shook it off until more people came flying to tell me. Now I felt like the entire senior class knew. I do not remember details of who, what, when, where, how. But I remember Ezekiel saying it was just a "friend kiss." I literally remember each emotion I had that day because it went from disbelief (no way would Ezekiel do this; he would not; how could he do this?) to feeling betrayed and deceived. I am not a jealous type, so I did not care that a few of my friends (not your aunties) would blatantly caress his abs in front of folks because I knew where his heart was. Plus I figure both parties (Ezekiel and some of the girls) just loved the attention. But that day, it went overboard. Maybe she really did like him; maybe she was jealous he liked me and was really trying to pursue him. Maybe all that attention and being in the limelight with girls finally got to him, and he gave in. Who knows? I will never know, nor do I care now, but right in that instant, my emotion changed to *done*. I never knew I was a savage until that day.

I got all the details and talked to them individually in a very mild-mannered way and simply ended a friendship with her (the friend who kissed Ezekiel). Unfortunately, since that was Scarlett's

BFF, she stopped being friends with me too. I ended the friendship not because of the kiss but because of the attitude she came with, as she felt she had done no wrong. Yes, she was a friend of mine, not a best friend but surely not an acquaintance. She had a boyfriend, and so I thought she would understand. Her boyfriend did not attend the school at the time, and so I wondered if that played a role in her actions. Was she looking for some love and affection? Or was it a mistake, or did people misinterpret the kiss? To this day, I have no idea, but I did not care at the moment. I respected her as a friend and as a female but not after that day.

Then I dealt with Ezekiel. My mind was made and set, and there was no going back. Honestly, I did not want to end my friendship; I mean, who wants to end a friendship over a guy...no girl who understands the *girl code*: chicks over dicks all the way. Yet I felt I needed to because she felt she did not do anything wrong. Instead of apologizing, she was confronting me like I was crazy and in the wrong. Second, I did not have the time or the patience to sit and try to converse with her about a guy I knew was done in my mind and heart. Time is valuable, girls. Time is something that cannot be given back. It cannot be stopped or erased; it keeps going, so if you stay stuck and do not move along with time, you are going to get left behind. Okay, so I literally had to just ignore my old girlfriend because it was just negative and sometimes hostile energy. Trust me, many people, especially my BFFs, wondered why I did not go off on her or fight her. Well, first off, I was not fighting, definitely not over this situation. Second, I was not her girlfriend; I was Ezekiel's girlfriend. I chose him to be my first *official* boyfriend. It was him I was dating, not her. Yes, it takes two to tango, but if he was *my man*, he should have known better and not even be in a situation that ended like this. I know, so dramatic. Looking back, I should have squashed the beef or issue. I should have tried to talk it out with my friend. It was my pride and the feeling of being hurt that would not allow me to "forfeit." Nobody is perfect—no man and no woman. We all make mistakes. I am glad we were able to look past it after high school because girlfriend breakups are worse than boyfriend break ups. I believe I could have worked it out with Ezekiel also. If we were both willing to work at making sure it never happens again, and God said "yes, make it work," it might have happened. However, I was immature and too self-absorbed.

However, I do believe in working together in a relationship because best believe grass ain't greener on the other side. Yet your grass can be greener if you water it daily and pull them weeds out.

Anyway, I looked at it differently. I felt like I took a leap, a chance on him, a guy no one in my circle even noticed before. I am not saying I got him out of his box, but he went from wearing Led Zeppelin shirts to Hollister. He went from Star Wars club innovator to the hottest guy every girl wanted to touch. Nothing bad, but he changed, and I think he knew it too. I think a part of me wanted a reason or a sign to show me whether or not he was *the one*. Yes, a part of me was on cloud nine. He was different, and yea, I felt different (in my 2 Chainz voice). We might have been meant for one another. We clicked on another level. Yet the witty and charming, outspoken guy from my AP classes shattered my heart. He let me down. But I did not show it. I bottled it up. I controlled my emotions. I showed no emotion. I was a professional by now because of all my emotional breakdowns I had with Titus. I knew better now.

I broke up with him without a tear on that same day, not at school though. I drove to his house and just ended it in my car. I honestly remember feeling nothing. He stormed out of my car, and I drove off. Did I cry? Yes, but I definitely did not show anyone. On the flip side, Ezekiel was destroyed. I mean, people would literally come to me and ask me to make it better, and I would remind them that he kissed another girl. Later in life, he told me many of the guys, especially the football players, gave him so much crap because he messed up. He said I was the "it" girl, and he screwed up. Not going to lie; I did feel good knowing some of the guys I used to talk to had my back and defended me. I mean not to make him feel bad, but these guys had a heart and were on my side. Rather than just being on his side because they are male, they saw me and the situation and felt I was in the right. I did not like seeing him in pain and in such turmoil, but there was no going back. I think we tried being friends, but of course, that was hard too.

## *Prom*

With a fresh breakup and still having some feelings and little quirky things that are only between us, it was odd, but somehow, we decided to go to senior prom together. Not sure if that was a good or bad choice on his end, but I look back now, and I am glad I went with him even if we may not have enjoyed ourselves. I say that because he was my first official boyfriend, so it is fitting. If I went with anyone else such as Titus who, of course, was right back in my life, I do not know how things would have played out emotionally, physically, mentally, and spiritually. Like I said, Titus was always in and out of my life, and you already know how much of an impact he had on me, and he knew 100 percent. So if I went to prom with him, my emotions might have been in a whirlwind, and who knows. However, I thank God 100 percent that he did not let that happen. I honestly think it was God. Beyoncé's song, "You turned out to be the best thing I never had," is literally my theme song for Titus. Crazy because I remember feeling like "Make It Last Forever" by Keith Sweat when I would just be in his presence. Lord, the whirling emotions and feelings of a teen!

Speaking of music, the music you listen to definitely affects you. When I would go out with my girls to "turn up," we would listen to ratchet music because we already knew what we had in mind, and it was not to go to church. The same thing applies to feelings, especially as a hormonal teen. You hear love songs and think you understand and feel it, and it pulls you in. You are either crying a river and feeling bad for yourself or saying, "*Independent*" and "I don't need a man." That is why, my loves, I listen to gospel music all the time now, whether I am driving in my car or working out. The songs about His love makes me cry in the most beautiful way. The revelations I have when I am in that music are always uplifting and the truth. Lastly, it is always what my Father wants me to feel. I am not saying stop listening to all music but Christian music. No, that is impossible, and I would never impose that. I just want you to be aware of what you are putting into your body and soul, not just food wise but what you are listening to and subconsciously absorbing. However, I ain't gon' lie; the R & B music and the random pop love songs were definitely poppin', and I do not think they make them like that anymore, but I am biased being raised in the best era. But all I know is the love songs written about the Great I Am are the everlasting and most impactful ones to this day...because "His love never fails, it never gives up, and it never runs out on me."

## High school is slipping away

They say "pussy is power." However, in high school, I did not see it that way or believe it. I saw it the other way around. I saw and thought that once you have sex with a male, it is over. I am talking about your first time. After the first time, I thought it loses its value, meaning you are now stuck on it or that person. But because you have given your first time to that special person, there is immediately a special bond created, or so you want there to be. I have seen girls go through it because after they give it up and things don't go well, they are devastated. They basically believed he was *the one*, and it becomes heartbreaking when it looks like it is not. I mean, they were doing anything and everything to make it work. Shoot! Not going to lie, but that scared me. I was like, "*Heck, no!*" I do not ever want to feel like I gave the most important thing to a person, only for them to open it and toss it like a pair of worn socks. No, thank you! I'll wait. I felt like it gave the guy power over her. I do not think anyone should have that much power, especially not a young boy who does not even know what he wants to eat for lunch. I said, "Nope." This is God's temple anyway. I will keep it for God and His will. Oh, and I was also deathly afraid of pregnancy and STDs. I was so afraid of pregnancy and STDs that I didn't even want to get too close to a real penis, no matter how much I liked him. I know there are ways to have protected sex, but it does not keep you away from STDs (sexually transmitted diseases).

When I found that some had no cure, I was even more grossed out. I wanted to ask the guys, "Do you have a recent blood check to make sure you are good?" I am not saying everyone who has sex has STDs, but what I rationalized was that if you are having sex with multiple partners, the chances of catching it is way higher than if you just do not participate in the act, period. When guys and girls questioned why I was *saving* my virginity, I would tell them those were my reasons, but it was not my number one reason. I was honestly too ashamed at the time, but it was because I really believed in what God said in the Bible. I know it sounds like Miss Goody Two-shoes, but I was really a square. Yup, I sure was. Unfortunately, I was not confident about it or proud. It is now embarrassing to say that I could not admit that my dedication and faith in Jesus made me hold onto my virginity. It almost reminds me of how Jesus told Peter that he would deny Him three times, and Peter was like, "Nope, I would never," and he did it three times in a row. Same. Here I was, denying it and trying to put it on practical things like society and peers—like I did not want to get pregnant or get STDs—but it was really the Holy Spirit keeping me in check. I told you that conviction has always been there from the beginning. By the way, later in life, I did learn that pussy is power, but I realized that when I was in college (you can read about that one after).

Back to prom; I am grateful for how prom went and with whom I spent it. I might have never told Ezekiel how grateful I was because we were not really on good terms, and maybe a part of me at the time was not fully present. But I did appreciate him. I knew how much he *loved* and cared for me, and he showed it, even until that night at prom. After prom, we went our separate ways—no glamorous hotel stay for me, nor a crazy prom after-party. I actually hung out with a random group of people, one of whom I had a crush on. Yup, you're probably thinking, *Moved on that fast?* No, a lot of my crushes were just infatuations; I was just physically attracted or intrigued, but that fades after I figure them out or if I find out I don't really care for them as a person and move on.

That night, I was having a conversation with this new crush, and I learned a lot about myself. While I was going through those emotional roller coasters, I realized that I did not view how others saw me. I am not saying you should care what other people think because you should not, but I think it is also not good to be so self-absorbed that you do not take the time to notice how others feel.

That night, he basically told me that he thought I was a slut, sleeping around with a lot of the guys who played football. Sadly, he thought this because of who I was around and who was in my circle. I am not going to lie; it hurt, but it also gave me a reality check. It may have been a little late, but better late than never. I honestly did care about what people thought about my character. I did not care that they thought I slept around because I know I did not, and all the boys they thought hit it knew they did not. However, I would never want to be seen as arrogant, selfish, or mean.

That night, I also realized that it would have been great to take the time to get to know everyone, not just the people that I played sports with or the guys I had the hots for. I wish I would have taken the time to talk to each peer, especially the ones I always saw in my classes over and over or the ones I never even had more than a conversation with due to a group activity. I say this not because I want to clear my name with each person or to be more popular. No, I honestly think it would have helped me understand that person, which would in turn help me understand myself much better. Remember, I loved getting to know these guys because I learned about what I liked and did not and saw a different view of them; in turn, I saw a different view of myself. In the same way, it would have been nice to see how others—not like myself and who I was not physically attracted to—may have provided a different perspective to life. I guess it happened for a reason, and I am learning from it.

In essence, I want you girls to take advantage. Talk to everyone; be kind always. I hope I was never mean to anyone, but again, everyone has their own perspective. High school can be harsh, and I remember peers making comments about how Asian people eat dogs or how our eyes slant in a different way, without thinking about how hurtful and offensive those words can be. I am not justifying any actions, but if I was associated in any way or did not stop anyone else from being mean, I am guilty. I feel like I should have been the one to stand up and stop situations if I ever were in any because I knew how it felt to feel like an outcast. *Bullying* was a little different when I went to school from what it is now. I feel that it was like a rite of passage in school, like you got made fun of no matter what. It can be from the clothes you are wearing to stereotypical things. I do not think it was out of malice but just a different way of showing love to another peer—well, sometimes at least, and sometimes it was hurtful. However, I think there is and was trauma from both parties that were involved. When I was younger, before my senior year, I was a lot more self-conscious and unable to stand up for myself and could not stand up for others.

Being made fun of is not something I want you to experience or partake in, and I pray God gives you the strength and wisdom to not only stand up for yourself but for others when necessary. If I ever offended anyone or hurt anyone because I was a part of that situation, I apologize from the depths of my soul because I know that cut can last a lifetime. I can remember that gut-wrenching feeling when people would put their index fingers on the side of their eyes and pull them apart to make me feel ugly and a little less of a human because my eyes looked different and how it frustrated me when they called me Chinese because all Asian people were "Chinese" to them. I will forever remember those words and those ill feelings that came with it. In fact, they either grow toward hate, or hopefully, it grows to understanding and healing. For a long time, it was hate—hate toward the people, hate toward myself. I think my faith was shaken. I did not like and did not understand why we had to move. Why did I have to feel isolated? Why did I have to leave what looked like a great situation for me? But thank God there was a silver lining. It did not happen overnight. It was and still is a process. Learning that the people who once hurt you were either ignorant or broken themselves gives you empathy.

However, true healing is a choice you make, and only through Jesus can I say I am in the process myself. Now I honestly laugh to myself when I hear about people from other cultures trying to "convert" themselves to being Korean or just fully indulge in Korean culture. I think it is beautiful and amazing that other cultures believe Korean customs and lifestyle is so cool, but I laugh because I know God is smiling down at me in those moments. You see, for the longest time when I was growing up, being Korean was not cool, and I was not proud of being Korean (I am embarrassed to admit). But now I feel like God and I have an inside joke because now it is embraced and loved all over the world. He basically said, "You best love yourself and who you are. The entire world caught up to it now. We're waiting on you." Just kidding. But for real, I can honestly say I love being me! I embrace my non-double eyelid, slanted eyes, my healthy yet noncurvaceous body. I love the stinky kimchi, pickled radishes, and everything above. I am proud to be Korean, born in Canada, yet raised in Los Angeles. Yet peeling back the layers and truly healing takes time and a lot of self-reflection. I am continuously learning in this process through the guidance of Christ but excited for more revelations to come.

## Grad night

Grad night was uneventful, to say the least. Although I had fun with friends, for some reason, everyone felt so far away. I thought it was the venue. We chose a random water park/arcade spot in Redlands or somewhere. We could not do Disneyland because our school was banned from the year before. I really wanted to go to Disneyland because all the seniors talked about how fun it was every year, but I never got to experience it. On the bright side, we would be with our graduating class and no one else, we thought. Yet when the night came, it was bleak. First, one of my BFFs was not allowed to go, and we were really bummed out about that. It had something to do with alcohol, but I mean, a lot of people did drink before we left, but she was one of the unlucky ones who got caught. So that was the start of it. Next, we got there, and it was cool, but as the night went on, I just kind of got bored. I do not know if it was because it was a huge place, and it almost felt empty or if I had too high expectations, and it was not met.

What I thought would be a nostalgic and beautiful night just made me feel sad and alone. I did not feel like I connected with everyone or had lasting memories with the entire group. If I could go back, I wish we made it more intimate. But I guess when you are a senior in high school, you want out. You think you got this and are ready to take on the world and so ready to say good riddance to high school. I was ready to take on the world, but I was also going to miss high school.

Yes, high school was not easy and had me at lows and highs, but I loved Bellflower as it molded me. I loved all the peers, staff, and coaches that helped shape me and impact my mindset and determination. I loved all the stupid little drama between teenage kids and the life lessons I learned on and off the court/field from playing sports. I learned how to be a good leader while also being a noble citizen. Some people want to forget high school because all they think of are the negatives, but I embraced it all. I know our high school was not perfect, and neither was I, but I do know God placed me there for a reason. I am in awe. He turned my worst transition, or so I thought, to the best thing that has ever happened to me. And for that, I am grateful. Nope, I did not graduate as valedictorian but proudly just as ASB president. I think I was like number seven in my class. It does not matter as you will learn it does not determine your success or how smart you actually are. In addition, after high school, what you do with all those grades and knowledge is what really counts. By the end of high school, I was definitely feeling myself. I had no idea what I wanted to do with my life, but I knew I wanted to help people. I was waiting for God's calling. My purpose: His will to be done. I walked across that stage with my head held high, and as I looked into the stands where my family sat and into the sky, I knew all was well. I was truly in bliss. I was proud of my achievements and stoked to see where God was going to take me next. All I had in my mind were thoughts and visions of my future, my future with no one or nothing in the way. Even if I may have come out of high school not knowing what I exactly wanted, I gained certainty of what I did not want. That, my darling, is a blessing on its own.

I went on to college nearby, played volleyball, and got to meet new friends, and of course, new guys came in the picture, and some old ones stayed. But that's a whole other book. Maybe you'll read when you are in high school. I will tell you about my transition from high school to college and all the in-between life lessons. There were even more rough patches, and just as I thought I went over one hurdle, there was a row full ahead of me. Also, the *game* does not end here. It also adapts and transitions with you. So it continues. The *game* ain't over, and the journey of life is just beginning.

What an ending, I know. I know a part of you may feel unsatisfied because it may not have been the ending you wanted. Trust me, I have watched enough coming-of-age high school love movies to totally understand what may have been expected. It usually ends with the girl and boy in love and happily ever after. But, my loves, I wrote this book for that reason. I wanted you to know everyone's teen life does not end as in the movies. Yet some do. They may have a beautiful and transitional relationship into adulthood and even marriage. However, even those couples go through trials and tribulations. Yet your own mother did not have that fairy-tale ending after high school. In fact, she had the total opposite. She was not in love, far from commitment, a little jaded, yet much more confident and ready to take on the next chapter in her life...college. For most of our life, we are so busy trying to make others (parents, family, etc.) happy and proud that we actually forget what makes us happy, what brings us joy, and what makes sense for us. We also forget that it should be about "how can I bring glory to God?" and not about me.

Trust me, I never would have thought this was how my high school life would end and how early adult life would start. I was used to having a set plan and checking off my list. But I realized you can plan and check the boxes, but if God ain't put it for you, it ain't for you. Plus you ain't gonna want it if God ain't in it. Yeah, a part of me would have liked to have had a *high school sweetheart* and a full-ride scholarship to a renowned university, knowing exactly what I wanted to major in and become. But I said, "Jesus, take the wheel." I could not hear exactly what way I was supposed to go, but I sure heard what He was telling me not to do. I am glad I had clarity and the faith to hear Him in my heart as He was always there to steer me in the path He made me. People say, "Listen to your heart, follow your heart," and many times in my youth, I did not get it. I could not hear what my heart said; all I heard were my thoughts and feelings and did not understand how it helped make life-changing decisions. However, I believe that phrase means listening to God and truly being able to hear what He has to say and obey Him. It is very difficult because many times, it may not make sense, and it may be something you may not want to do, but more so, in those moments, I know it is Him because it sure could not have come from my own thoughts. I now pray that He yells at me and shoves me when I ain't listening to His whispers so that I may continue on His path and not my own. But that is not like Him… "He whispers because He's close," as Tauren Wells sings. The Lord gives us the free will to make our own decisions.

Make sure to always make time for God. He needs to be your number one priority and not your last resort. I think when I would randomly run at night to the bleachers at Bellflower high or on the riverbed, it was my time with God, at my most vulnerable moment. I can be running the bleachers, overlooking the city, or at the beach looking at the endless sea. I can be happy or in despair. I can be in tears of heartache or in pure bliss. Whatever mood or whatever thoughts I had, I brought it to Him. Even though I may not say anything, it was during those times I was in my purest form. Just me and God. After every run, I would feel uplifted as if a weight was just lifted off my shoulders, and I felt free. I did not pray out loud or speak, but sometimes I feel like that was the best because I just wanted the Holy Spirit to take over, and He knew what I needed. It also had a lot to do with the fact I either listened to no music or gospel music. I wanted to be completely alone and in the space with Him so that He can bring clarity, and that was my therapy. People think I worked out to get fit, but it really was all for my mental, emotional, and spiritual health—free therapy. I probably needed and still need real therapy, but hey, that's all I knew and had the resources for. I want to stress how important that time was for me and pray that you girls will also find that special space with Him.

Of course, my life did not end with high school; it just started. The same goes with my love life. I took the lessons I learned in high school and *the game* that was molded in me and took it to the next level.

# AFTERWORD

Aubrey and Ava, I wrote this because I want to put myself out there in the most vulnerable position so that you will see that I have been there and done that. I also believe that seeing me open myself up and expose all of me will inspire you to always be honest with me and your dad about everything. Above all, I pray you are always honest with yourself. I remember Halbi always telling me to read books, yet he hated reading. I slowly realized as parents, you need to practice what you preach. As you girls saw me and Dad workout, you girls just automatically would try to exercise when we would be in the backyard. Then when I began to read books in front of you, I saw that it made you want to read on your own, and that is what I learned from you girls. Same with why you girls may love worship music as I would always have it on my radio and even when I am exercising. However, I also love how you girls know more R & B and pop songs than I do because of your dad. We must do what we want you to do, not just talk about it but be about it.

So through this book and through your own experiences with God and me and your dad, I hope you will understand what real unconditional love is for me. I hope this book helps you keep this opened door we have between us. Also, I pray you will always have a growing relationship with God as I have. I know because of the foundation I had with God, I was able to hear the Holy Spirit when He would bluntly say, "He ain't it," and how I recognized when He would send me visions and see how things would unfold amid a storm because of His grace. The *game* I hope you gained from all this is to *keep* God first. He is the foundation of who we are in the core, our spirit. "Trust in the Lord with all your heart and lean not on your own understanding" (Proverbs 3:5). He is "the way, the truth, and the life" (John 14:6). Don't you ever forget it. I pray that you are able to hear Him and listen to Him even when it is loud from other influences other than God trying to pull you away from what God wants for you and what your purpose is. "Devil gon' try and take me out of that church, but you can't take the church out of me," as Anne Wilson declares. He speaks directly to you. You just have to be willing and choose to open your heart to hear Him. I never understood people saying "listen to your heart" because I would be still and literally try to hear what my heart is saying to do, but the entire time, my heart was talking to me. I remember I loved the saying "persistence beats resistance" because to me, if you are persistent and never give up, you will get what you want. But now I see it differently. God is persistent, but if it is not His will, I do not want it, nor do I hope it is something I continue to be persistent about.

I also realized that I must pray to resist temptations of all levels so that we may be focused on His purpose. Remember, we would always pray that we would be able to embody the fruit of the spirit: love, joy, peace, patience, kindness, goodness, faithfulness, gentleness, and self-control (Galatians 5:22). Continue to strive for that and pray for it all day because if we all had these attributes and believe in Jesus, it would solve all our problems. Pastor Michael Todd from Transformation Church says it best, "The Bible is the only book that when you read it, it reads you." I believe it is the most important book we should read because it is our manual and needs to be used as a guide. I hope there are more churches and pastors like Pastor Mike and Transformation Church that can reach all people and be relatable because it is based on the Word. I am forever grateful to TC as they also helped me in this journey. In a time where I felt there was no more community and honesty in being a part of church, they came and breathed life and hope in me once again. I do not physically attend there but trust I am there emotionally and spiritually through every sermon. Hallelujah!

Be real. Be true. Keep it one hundred with everyone, especially yourself, because just like they say, game recognizes game…*real* recognizes *real*. Embrace your emotions and learn to understand them, but most importantly, learn to control your emotions. Feelings are normal, but know they evolve, especially during young teenage years. Emotions, if not controlled, can be detrimental.

For example, when you are angry and want to physically take it out on someone, which will only worsen the scenario, walk away. Then recalculate what you feel instead of acting on impulse. It can better help you resolve the underlying issue rather than make it worse. The flesh wants to act out on instant gratification and always wants to blame others, but true healing is none of the above. Controlling your emotions and feelings leads to controlling your mind. By doing so, you will be mastering your actions, which is killing two birds with one stone. If you can control your emotions and feelings, you control your mind, and controlling your body will be easy as it will become second nature and an important skill. For instance, your body and mind will be in sync, unlike Mr. R. Kelly.

All in all, I have a special place for the city of Bellflower. It is crazy because there was a time I hated this new city that I was forced to adapt to and move into. Yet God's plans were greater. My most valuable lessons and what made me *me* were all from here. I was formed and made my God, no doubt. Yet my characteristics were enhanced and molded through my experiences right here where God brought my family. I did not appreciate "here" back then, but now standing "here," I realize the importance that took place back there. My confidence and ability to speak out and say what is on my mind and in my heart, not to be scared to express myself, and to learn about myself while slowly embracing my true self were just some of the most vital parts that were ingrained in me. This city, my middle and high school, pushed out my boldness, my hustle-hard-at-all-times mentality, my swag, and my street smarts as I was still trying to hold onto my Korean Canadian Christian beliefs and culture. I know it was not the city or just the people but only through God's divine plan that all this unfolded the way it did, but I just want to point out that fifteen to twenty years later, looking back, I see it. I understand why everything happened the way it did. Yet at the time, it did not make sense, nor did I grasp God's amazing grace. I pray you enjoy every moment, both good and bad. Know for sure Jesus got you.

I also wrote this because as a parent, I hate seeing you in pain. If I could, I would take all the pain from you—the pain and suffering that is coming—and consume it in me so it would not touch you. God does not like seeing us hurt either, but it may be good for us because we learn from it and mold us. I also realized I gained "crazy faith," per Pastor Michael Todd, through it all, and if you don't go through your own trials and tribulations, you start to believe you got this and even think you don't need Him, your Lord and Savior. Therefore, I believe that it is good to go through difficult times. My job is not to protect you from harm's way (which is impossible) but to *prepare* you and show you what worked for me—Jesus. Only God can protect us. He has already won the battle. He did that. "He sent his one and only son Jesus to die for us so that we would not perish and have everlasting life" (John 3:16), where there is no pain and suffering.

One of my favorite phrases is "pain is weakness leaving the body," but in another perspective, as Lecrae says, "Pain strengthens, and fear drives faith." Believe that! I love you, girls! You have given me so much more than just being a momma. I cannot wait to share the next chapter of my life, college life and all the life lessons I accumulated. All my trials and tests have now become part of my testimony. I know my testimony was given to me to give all the *glory* to Him, to show what He did for me and how it has snowballed all throughout my young adult life. It is part of His purpose and His will for me. Therefore, I am sharing it with not only you but to whomever else needs to hear this. It is not coincidence that you read this, but I believe there were parts where you felt that tug in your heart. I pray this will only bring you a step closer to building a relationship with Jesus Christ. My story does not conclude here. It continued to evolve and continues to progress to this day. As one of our favorites, Tauren Wells, says, "God's not done with you… It's not over. It's only begun."

"God's not done writing your story."

# ABOUT THE AUTHOR

Grace Chang Piggue is a wife and mother of two young daughters. After high school, she transitioned to Long Beach City College and continued to play volleyball there. She then transferred to California State University–Dominguez Hills where she obtained her bachelor's degree in human services. Shortly after, she felt a push from God to continue pursuing higher education and got her masters of science in occupational therapy, again at CSUDH. She has always wanted to *help* others but never truly understood what her purpose was and what His will was for her...until now.